# PRAISE FOR
# NAMELESS BUT KNOWN

*Nameless but Known* is a theologically rich exploration of Christ's matchless mercy. With biblical precision and keen insight, Tamar Miller brings to life six unnamed women in the Gospels who encountered Jesus in their deepest moments of need. Through these narratives, Tamar reminds us that God's mercy is not only for those with prominence, but it also extends to the forgotten, the broken, and the unseen. This book is an invitation to trust in the Redeemer who knows each of us by name. A must-read for those longing to grasp the depths of God's compassion and grace.
—**Whitney Eaton**, director of Ministry to Women, Providence Church, Frisco, TX (www.providencefrisco.com)

*\*\*\**

*Nameless but Known* is a beautifully written and deeply insightful biblical exploration of God's love and mercy through the stories of six unnamed women in the Gospels. With biblical depth, practical wisdom, and thoughtful reflection, Tamar Miller invites readers to see themselves in these stories—to recognize that they are seen, known, and deeply loved by Christ. Through this book, you will be encouraged by the transforming power of God's mercy and reminded that your story is still unfolding in His hands. Read *Nameless but Known* and be inspired to grow in your understanding of God's unwavering love and grace.
—**Mark Bricker**, discipleship pastor, McGregor Baptist Church, Fort Myers, FL (www.mcgregor.net)

*\*\*\**

As I have encountered women all over the world, I have realized we have one significant need in common: we desire to be known, really known. Knowing comes from the tender protection and provision that we can only get from our Heavenly Father, who not only knows us and

our circumstances, but knows our hearts' greatest need as well. In *Nameless but Known*, Tamar Miller reminds us of the mercy we have through the Gospel and the lovingkindness of Jesus to know us and change hearts and lives like only He can. This insightful book's message is one to repeat to yourself over and over, and to share with a friend.
—**Sarah Lightner,** missionary with Family Legacy Missions International, author of www.thebiblicallymindedfamily.com, Arcadia, FL (www.familylegacy.com)

\*\*\*

You are seen, known, and loved by Jesus! In *Nameless but Known*, Tamar Miller leads us to discover layers and layers of the complete story of Jesus' compassion and love toward women and how much He cares for us. In the process, we are challenged to look deeper into our own souls to examine our level of compassion toward the lost, as well as toward the household of faith, so that our response to life's challenges is not trite or superficial. Be prepared to examine yourself and be grateful for our merciful God!
—**Linda Montgomery,** Stonecroft Ministries Regional Representative, Prosper, TX (www.stonecroft.org)

\*\*\*

This book, *Nameless but Known*, draws you into the lives of six women whose names were never given in the biblical text, but we can all relate to them. Tamar Miller has the unique ability to encourage the reader as she walks us through Scripture to witness the extravagant grace and mercy of the Savior Jesus Christ, who sees past the flaws of these women, and therefore can see *us*...beyond our flaws. His only desire is that we repent and follow Him.
—**Kai Shanks,** McGregor Baptist Church Women's Ministry Teacher, co-coordinator Hope4Kidz Haiti Mission, Fort Myers, FL (www.rmibridge.org)

# Nameless but Known

Six biblical women Jesus met with His mercy

Written by

Tamar Miller

Published by KHARIS PUBLISHING, an imprint of KHARIS MEDIA LLC.

Copyright © 2025 Tamar Miller

ISBN: 978-1-63746-332-1

ISBN: 1-63746-332-4

Library of Congress Control Number: 2025940419

Cover Design by Jeff Eskridge, 239Creative.com

All rights reserved. This book or parts thereof may not be reproduced in any form, stored in a retrieval system, or transmitted in any form by any means - electronic, mechanical, photocopy, recording, or otherwise - without prior written permission of the publisher, except as provided by United States of America copyright law.

Unless otherwise noted, all Scripture quotations are taken from the Christan Standard Bible®, Copyright © 2017 by Holman Bible Publishers. Used by permission. Christian Standard Bible® and CSB© are federally registered trademarks of Holman Bible Publishers.

All KHARIS PUBLISHING products are available at special quantity discounts for bulk purchase for sales promotions, premiums, fund-raising, and educational needs. For details, contact:

Kharis Media LLC
Tel: 1-630-909-3405
support@kharispublishing.com
www.kharispublishing.com

*This book is dedicated with thankfulness*

*to three cherished fathers of daughters*

*whose lives have been changed by God's matchless mercy:*

*To my dad, Ralph*

*and*

*To my stepdad, Bill*

*and*

*In memory of my dad-in-law, Troy (aka: Papel)*

# Acknowledgements of Appreciation

I am tremendously appreciative for the opportunity to write and publish a second book, even though it was not an easy undertaking; therefore, I offer words of deep gratitude to multiple individuals for their help in making a book idea become an exciting reality. I recognize there may be unnamed persons not included below, but who should be, who kindly provided much needed prayer, suggestions, support, encouragement, and even presented different perspectives throughout the duration of this project. To you, I want to say…Thank you very, very much! In addition, I want to convey my sincere thankfulness to…

<u>My Heavenly Father and Savior Jesus</u>: Apart from You and the indwelling Holy Spirit, I can do nothing; but with You, so much is possible, and You continue to amaze me. I cannot express adequate words to thank you for the way in which You have graciously extended Your compassionate care and tender mercy—though undeserved—toward me and my family. I pray this book will glorify You and encourage readers to grow in their desire to follow You through a deeper study of Your Word. Thank You, Lord God!

<u>My husband, David, and sons, Anthony and Carson</u>: Thank you for your patience, love, and unwavering support during this writing project. I am so proud of all three of you. David, I am extremely grateful for your valuable feedback and editing suggestions each time I dropped another manuscript page on your lap to read. I also appreciate your faithful prayers on my behalf during many overwhelmed moments. Thank you, guys, for your permission to include personal stories about our family within this book. Perhaps a glimpse into our

story will encourage other families with hope to continue to trust God's matchless mercy.

My mom and friend, Sharon: I appreciate your wisdom, guidance, prayers, suggestions, and overall support of this second book. You have brought such encouragement, and I am pleased to share this writing journey with you. Thank you for being my honorary agent and consistently sharing my first book with your church family and friends out in Texas. That means so much to me!

MBC Women's Ministry Teaching Team: Krisztina, Julie, and Kai, what a blessing that this book developed from a Bible study series that we previously taught together. Thank you for your beneficial feedback, prayers, and support. I am grateful to serve alongside you weekly in the women's ministry.

Jeff at 239Creative: Once again, you have been a remarkable addition to this second book project with your creative ideas, editing guidance, marketing concepts, and inspirational talent demonstrated through the book cover development, website material, and video promotion. Thank you so much!

MBC Ministerial Staff and Life Group: I am grateful for your prayers, support, love, biblical insight, humor, accountability, and the weekly opportunity to gather with you as a church family to celebrate Jesus and study God's Word together. You have shown me mercy in more ways than I deserve, so thank you.

My "Special Moms" Support Group: I appreciate the inspirational and transparent stories you frequently share with me about your experiences in caring for children with special needs. I am grateful to share meals together and pray for each other, as we rely on the Lord for our special kids. There is a chapter included in this book that is dedicated especially to you. I pray it will encourage you.

Donna: My faithful friend, coworker, and avid prayer warrior, thank you for your encouragement and support throughout this project. I appreciate your words of wisdom and your example of tenacious determination, unwavering trust in our Savior, devotion to your family and friends, and your remarkable kindness. Everyone should have at least one friend like you.

Becca Buddy: You are a blessing to our family and an answer to prayer in serving for multiple years as an adult buddy to our son who lives with disability. Your intentional care of him during weekly church activities has allowed him to participate in the MBC student ministry, without his embarrassing parents hanging around. Thank you for the way you love, respect, and include him.

Carly Rose Photography: Thank you for providing your photographic expertise for the author photo included on the back covers for both of my published books. I appreciate it.

Kharis Media Publishing Team: Thank you again for your willingness to collaborate with me to publish a second book for the wonderful purpose of telling others about Jesus and His Gospel message. I appreciate all the ways you provided the necessary guidance and valuable materials to partner with me in the publishing and promoting process. A special thanks to the Kharis project manager and book editor, James and Mary, who kindly assisted me with this writing endeavor.

All Cherished Readers: I love to read, and I love to write, so I am grateful to have another written resource released that is an extension of what the Lord has called me to do, which is teaching about Jesus through a study of God's Word. It brings me great joy that you would choose to pick up a book with my name attached to it. May you be encouraged by studying stories of other similar people who lived in earlier times and encountered the merciful Savior. They remind us of our need today for the same Savior, whose name is Jesus.

<u>Lastly, in memory of my dear college friend, Jill</u>: Our friendship flourished for 35 memorable years throughout multiple seasons of life, until her heavenly Savior welcomed her home on 1/19/25, following an almost 10-year battle with a rare neurological disease. Jill requested to travel this publishing road with me, even though we lived miles apart. She was excited about this second book, but sadly, did not get to see its completion. She was deeply loved and will be sorely missed.

# Contents

Introduction .................................................................... 13

Chapter 1: The Mark And Measure Of Mercy ............................. 19

Chapter 2: The Divorced Woman By The Well ........................... 25

Chapter 3: The Adulterous Woman At The Center ...................... 43

Chapter 4: The Maternal Woman Within The Region ................. 60

Chapter 5: The Sinful Woman Around The Town ....................... 76

Chapter 6: The Disabled Woman In The Synagogue ................... 93

Chapter 7: The Widowed Woman Outside The City ................. 110

Conclusion .................................................................... 127

Scripture Index .............................................................. 132

# Introduction

❖

*God is merciful and the source of all mercy, and the Father of mercies and the God of all comfort, so that nothing can make Him any more merciful than He has always been.*[1]*

A women's ministry conference assembled within the sanctuary of a small church located in a region of Africa, and the diverse group of women gathered, worshiping the Lord prior to hearing a biblical message. I was one of the American guest speakers invited to teach a passage from God's Word to encourage this body of female believers in their journey of faith with the Lord. Later that day, however, I realized I was unprepared for the personal test of faith which the Lord utilized to further my own understanding of His matchless mercy and compassionate care.

I was on the platform with the other scheduled speakers at the front of the worship center, but could not see beyond the crowd of women. Upon hearing the singing of the conference participants, an unidentified stranger had slipped into the back of the sanctuary. As she made her way slowly down the aisle, I observed a bundled infant she carried in her arms. I assumed she was a latecomer to the conference

---

[1] A.W. Tozer and James L. Snyder, *The Quotable Tozer: A Topical Compilation of the Wisdom and Insight of A.W. Tozer* (Minneapolis, MN: Bethany House, 2018), 214-216. *Each chapter contains an opening quote from A.W. Tozer, except the conclusion chapter.

and was seeking an empty seat. What occurred next will forever remain etched in my memory.

This young mother courageously approached the platform and spoke quietly to the church pastor who was standing near the front. He was also the designated translator for the teaching time, and his wife was a respected leader within their women's ministry. When the worship song ended, the gathered group remained standing while the pastor shared the reason for this unknown woman's unusual presence. She was desperate, in need of assistance, and did not know what else to do or whom to turn to for help. She made the choice to step out into an unfamiliar crowd looking for salvation within a church setting.

The baby she embraced was dying from whooping cough. Perhaps this mother had unsuccessfully sought help from a doctor, or maybe she lacked sufficient funds to pay for medical services. None of us were familiar with her background, her family status, or her religious affiliation. All we could observe was a despairing mother who was drawn to seek the Lord God among His assembled people, and who bore a distressed plea for the healing of her helpless infant. The background of this suffering woman's plight was that she had previously buried two other children who had died from this same illness. The pastor quickly instructed us that we would momentarily stop the conference agenda to earnestly pray for this child and the grieving mother. The names of both the mom and her baby were never mentioned, but God knew who these two individuals were. He was aware of where they had come from, what they had endured, and what they needed. Providentially, the merciful Father used this conference setting to usher a helpless and hopeless woman into His presence, surrounded by caring Christ-followers to remind her of His lovingkindness.

I was overwhelmed by this remarkable scene, since at the time my two sons were just toddlers with reasonable access to medical resources that could prevent such an occurrence. Prior to the church family petitioning God on behalf of this afflicted infant, the tormented mother laid down her child upon the center of the platform in front of all of us, and then stepped to the side. This unknown, disheartened woman demonstrated a public surrender of her precious child—the weight of her world—into the faithful hands of her baby's Creator. She simply trusted Him to do what no one else could. **Hebrews 4:16** exhorts, **"Therefore, let us approach the throne of grace with boldness, so that we may receive mercy and find grace to help us in time of need."**

Until that moment, I had never witnessed, nor been called upon to pray for a stranger in such dire need. I pondered if I would have the courage, strength, and faith to do what this heroic mother had done if in the same position. In **Isaiah 49:13-16**, the sovereign Lord spoke to those in desperation who felt abandoned and forgotten: **"For the Lord has comforted His people, and will have compassion on His afflicted ones...Can a woman forget her nursing child, or lack compassion for the child of her womb? Even if these forget, yet I will not forget you. Look, I have inscribed you on the palms of My hands; your walls are continually before Me."**

After the congregation had finished praying for the ill child, the room became silent. We all watched and waited for what the sorrowful mom would do next. We hoped that God would miraculously intervene in the life of this newborn. As quickly as the mother had entered the sanctuary, she swiftly picked up her baby from the stage and walked up the aisle toward the exit doors. I never saw that woman again; I never received confirmation whether her baby lived or died, but God knows and that is what makes all the difference.

Through various tests and trials over time, I have learned that nothing compares to knowing God through His Word and being known by God. Yet how often do we question if the Lord understands the difficulties we are facing? Are we tempted to doubt whether the

Savior cares for us? Why do we struggle trusting God's mercy, which changes lives?

Perhaps you have found yourself surrounded by a group of people, but felt alone in your struggle. Maybe you have questioned whether God is aware of your suffering or cares about your loved ones. How do you respond when brought to the brink of despair? Where do you seek help for a dilemma? How do you cope with your fears or anxiety? The New Testament records multiple stories of people just like you and me who experienced the complex effects of living in a broken world. In God's Word, we read about those who hungered for compassion, thirsted for comfort, desired to receive mercy, yearned to be loved, but perhaps struggled to believe in God and trust His Word. In addition, many failed to extend mercy to others, when given the chance. You may find you can relate to their personal stories more than you imagined.

For instance, can you understand the agony a widowed woman felt, or grasp the quandary of a divorced woman, or empathize with the challenges endured by a disabled woman? Perhaps you can better identify with the troubles of an adulterous woman, or sympathize with the predicament of a woman marked by a defiled reputation, or relate to a despairing mother's concern over her child's recurring problems. What do these anonymous females have in common? Their stories are in the Bible, but surprisingly, their names are never disclosed. The Gospels provide details of the plight of each unidentified, but desperate woman coping with suffering, hardship, and discouragement. Each overlooked woman recognized the difficulty that came with being in a crowd, but feeling lost and alone... until she encountered Jesus, the merciful Savior. He noticed each woman and responded to her by demonstrating tremendous care and compassion, thus bringing hope for her future.

The purpose of this book, *Nameless but Known*, is to explore portions of Scripture within the four Gospel accounts and discover the power of God's matchless mercy extended toward six unidentified women, hidden among the crowd, yet seen and known by Christ. Their uplifting stories will remind you that the Lord God sees, hears, knows, understands, and cares for individuals; you too are not forgotten by Him (**Exodus 2:23-25**). I will encourage you to seek to know Jesus better by studying the Bible and remaining open to His teaching. I will also remind you that the sovereign Savior remains faithful throughout every generation to extend His magnificent mercy to undeserving persons in need of redemption. Their personal names might not be revealed to us, but each of them is certainly known by the only One who matters for eternity, Jesus Christ. **"Lord, You have searched me and known me" (Psalm 139:1)**.

# Chapter 1

## THE MARK AND MEASURE OF MERCY

*The Scriptures abound with the truth that God is a merciful God. Mercy is something that God is, it is a facet of His unitary being.*

In 2019, a hymns album, *His Mercy Is More*©, was released.[2] I became familiar with this music compilation when my husband recommended that I listen to these worship songs in my vehicle whenever I was out and about. At first, the melodic collection of songs did not catch my attention, nor sound different than other inspirational gospel music. Then, my youngest son requested to hear this soundtrack every morning on our drive to school. The more I listened to the biblically-based lyrics for each recorded hymn, the more I realized these worship songs were telling the dynamic story of the matchless mercy of God toward an undeserving sinner, and I was hooked. Though Christ-followers typically gather weekly within a worship service setting to proclaim the mercy of God, I can't help but wonder whether the church body's thankful testimony from Sunday morning translates into

---

[2] Matt Boswell and Matt Papa, *His Mercy Is More – The Hymns of Matt Boswell and Matt Papa, Vol 1* (Brentwood, TN: Integrity Music).

compassion in action by its members throughout the following weekdays.

How well do believers embrace God's mercy with gratitude and then extend much-needed mercy to others? The gift of mercy is designed to be an intentional expression of compassion in action; it is neither passive, nor simply an optional suggestion for the one who claims to be a child of God. Nevertheless, I admit my own weekly struggle with exhibiting gratitude and extending mercy and compassion to others, which is why I am so thankful for God's Word and my church family that regularly remind me of God's abundant, though undeserved, mercy through Christ.

Believers rightly speak of the redemptive grace of God when sharing the gospel message of Jesus and how it transforms lives. God proclaims His unmerited favor through offering the free gift of salvation to the unworthy sinner by faith in Christ alone. Yet, the matchless mercy of God is the other side of that same priceless coin, which has the power to change lives as well. The Lord provides His righteous justice and extends compassion to a depraved but repentant individual, who may not get what they justly deserve, even though they transgressed God's law. For the redeemed, Jesus paid the ransom for sin's penalty on their behalf by His sacrificial death on the cross. How grateful I am that God's great mercy through Jesus covers my many sins.

The Bible explains in **Ephesians 2:1-5**: **"And you were dead in your trespasses and sins in which you previously walked according to the ways of this world...We too all previously lived among them in our fleshly desires, carrying out the inclinations of our flesh and thoughts, and we were by nature children under wrath as the others were also. But God, who is rich in mercy, because of His great love that He had for us, made us alive with Christ even though we were dead in trespasses. You are saved by grace!"**

As we study six different New Testament stories of *Nameless but Known* biblical women who encountered Jesus and experienced His matchless mercy within their personal crises, it is helpful to first understand the multi-faceted characteristics of mercy. The benefits of mercy may grant a just pardon, advocate on another's behalf, or speak words that build up rather than tear down. Mercy may include forgiving an offense and not holding a grudge. The Bible exhorts believers to not give up when ministering to others, since we have been shown mercy ourselves through Jesus for the glory of God within the church (**2 Corinthians 4:1**). Furthermore, mercy granted is directly connected to the mercy giver, not solely dependent on the mercy recipient.

The Lord's matchless mercy is uniquely rich and loving, unrivaled, and beyond comparison, but also necessary and typically desired, since it brings hope. In **Isaiah 46:5**, the Lord God asks, **"To whom will you compare Me or make Me equal? Who will you measure Me with, so that we should be like each other?"** Moreover, God's Word in **Lamentations 3:22-23** proclaims that because of God's faithful love, His abundant mercies are new every morning. Nevertheless, we tend to forget, or perhaps dismiss, how remarkable and widespread is the compassionate care and kindness of Jesus. The holy standard for the mark and measure of mercy originates with our risen Savior. His example shown throughout His earthly ministry is designed to be imitated by the church body to further impact others for Christ. **Luke 6** records a sermon Jesus preached to a gathered crowd in which He taught them about the value of interpersonal relationships. In **verse 31**, Jesus provided a basic rule of thumb: **"Just as you want others to do for you, do the same for them."** The point being, if you desire another person to show mercy and compassion to you, then begin by extending mercy and kindness to that individual.

Since Christ-followers are called to live for and emulate Christ—albeit not always easy—this includes demonstrating compassion toward others, especially as grateful mercy-recipients themselves. Jesus also taught, **"Be merciful, just as your Father also is merciful" (Luke 6:36)**. Genuine mercy translates into selfless action, but often we fail to extend mercy to others, whether within our own households, church memberships/families, work environments, school classrooms, or toward our next-door neighbors. Exercising mercy tends to be a challenging choice, an unnatural act of sacrifice to provide for the well-being of another. Sometimes it's inconvenient, other times it's painful, and occasionally it's costly. Still, offering kindness and compassion to someone in need, whether deserving or not, is a treasured decision by the one in a position to grant mercy. If we are honest, we all desire the offer of mercy to us, specifically in our worst hour or in our most awful day. What a difference practicing mercy could make!

**Exodus 34:6-7**, describes the Lord God in this way: **"The Lord is a compassionate and gracious God, slow to anger and abounding in faithful love and truth, maintaining faithful love to a thousand generations, forgiving iniquity, rebellion, and sin."** Through His Son Jesus, our heavenly Father has ultimately demonstrated His faithful love with His forgiveness for our plaguing sin problem. God's lovingkindness, personified in Christ, stands as the hallmark of quintessential mercy, measured by His far-reaching compassion, and beyond compare.

Strangely, offering mercy appears simple, yet remains complex; it might even seem nonsensical to a casual observer. For example, mercy is shown if a guilty person does not receive the just punishment they deserve. It is a display of mercy if a debt-ridden person receives a financial gift to cover what they owe. Sometimes the results of acts of mercy are not appreciated by a surprised spectator, unless you are the fortunate individual upon whom mercy is bestowed.

Let me pose a couple questions: Do you and I prepare ourselves to extend mercy to another person if the opportunity arises? Do you and I ready ourselves to accept mercy with gratitude when we need it from someone else? The *Holman Concise Bible Dictionary* describes "mercy, merciful" in this way:

> Personal characteristic of care for the needs of others…closely tied to the compassion and pity of family relationships, which provide image for God's mercy…In the NT, mercy expressed strong emotional feelings, particularly of compassion and affection…God's mercy is shown in His readiness to forgive the penitent sinner and in the atoning work of Christ…Jesus Christ is the ultimate manifestation of God's mercy.[3]

The late theologian and author J. Dwight Pentecost used to say that mercy was "God's ministry to the miserable." Pastor and author Chuck Swindoll wrote about God's mercy:

> It is both intensely personal and immensely practical. For when I am treated unfairly, God's mercy relieves my bitterness. When I grieve over loss, it relieves my pain and anger and denial. When I struggle with disability, it relieves my self-pity. When I endure physical pain, it relieves my hopelessness. When I deal with being sinful, it relieves my guilt.[4]

---

[3] Trent C. Butler, editor, *Holman Concise Bible Dictionary* (Nashville, TN: Broadman & Holman Publishers, 2001), 421-422.

[4] Charles R. Swindoll, *The Tale of the Tardy Oxcart and 1,501 Other Stories* (Nashville, TN: Word Publishing, 1998), 237.

The Apostle Paul understood and appreciated God's irrefutable mercy when he conveyed in **1 Timothy 1:15-16, "This saying is trustworthy and deserving of full acceptance: 'Christ Jesus came into the world to save sinners' – and I am the worst of them. But I received mercy for this reason, so that in me, the worst of them, Christ Jesus might demonstrate His extraordinary patience as an example to those who would believe in Him for eternal life."**

God's matchless mercy can draw a broken unbeliever to Himself and also minister to the believer. No doubt about it, the magnitude of the Lord's mercy is far-reaching. It holds the power to change lives for the glory of God; to personally change your life and my life, too. I am grateful that the Bible shares details of multiple historical women who perhaps were not remembered by many, but were each uniquely known by Christ. I have selected six biblical narratives to study within *Nameless but Known,* each pointing to the majesty and mercy of the Lord God, who remains faithful throughout all generations.

In the chapters ahead, I present each unnamed woman's story with a basic format that will invite you to: (1) read the biblical account; (2) consider the context and details of the narrative; (3) contemplate the compassionate care demonstrated by Christ; (4) receive practical application; (5) think through a few questions tied to the story, and (6) explore further findings of God's mercy in other scripture passages. In addition, you will be reminded of the phenomenal gospel of grace through Jesus, for it tells the mercy-filled message that the Lord saves sinners because of His abundant kindness and extraordinary love toward broken and fallen mankind (**Titus 3:4-5**). May the Lord God continue to have mercy on us!

# Chapter 2

# THE DIVORCED WOMAN BY THE WELL

*Out of God's goodness flows His mercy...There is no limit to His mercy...We are all recipients of God's mercy. We think we are not, but we are.*

Do you recall the last time you engaged in an impromptu conversation with another person? Perhaps it involved a friend, family member, coworker, neighbor, or even a stranger, and included any number of random topics. The unexpected chat may have been sudden; you might have felt unprepared for the dialogue and were left to improvise, or maybe you quickly dismissed the opportunity altogether. Typically, this can happen if the brief conversation deals with political or religious matters. A conversation like that may be unique, but it is not unusual. If God has saved you, how well-prepared are you for engaging in an on-the-spot spiritual discussion about Jesus and the gospel message of salvation? How intentional are you to initiate such a spontaneous encounter? I was faced with these questions when I traveled to Greece in 2023 with a small mission's team. We met up with a couple of missionaries who were commissioned to spread the Good News in an area that had rarely been receptive to the biblical teachings of Jesus.

Depending on the city to which we traveled in Greece, many of the citizens were fluent in English, while others were eager to practice their minimal English language skills, especially if it meant mingling with an American visitor. While visiting a local library, I bumped into one such resident, a kind and friendly teenaged girl. She had been studying with a friend at the linked learning center when our paths crossed. As a mom of two teenagers myself, it seemed fitting to start the spontaneous conversation with this girl about the topic of education. She was finishing high school and was enthusiastically interested in attending college in the United States. This led to an exchange of questions and answers between us about family members, personal interests, and even religious affiliations, which opened the door for an intentional discussion about spiritual matters.

This young woman's parents, cultural, and religious upbringing had strongly influenced her, but had not included Christianity or the Bible. She admitted she had recently been questioning what she had been taught to believe about God. Her curiosity about the Bible and receptiveness to hearing more about Jesus were refreshing. I was grateful for a biblically-based gospel-tract resource, printed in her native language, to assist me in telling her the Good News of Christ in our spontaneous interaction. In addition, I simply shared my personal testimony of how God's mercy had changed my life through Christ. She was unfamiliar with the compassionate Savior. She had not heard how He loved and cared for individuals from all nations, and was sent to seek and save the lost—like an inquisitive adolescent residing in Greece.

It piqued the interest of this girl that Jesus was described as the One who generously offered His redemptive gift of grace by faith for eternal life to anyone who would repent and believe in Him, and that it was not a gift earned by a well-meaning person's endless religious works that inevitably fell short. She was uncertain of what to make of God's Son, quietly processing the new information I shared with her; yet she wanted to know more about Jesus, so I continued telling His story. After only chatting with this young woman for a short time, my heart was burdened for her spiritual well-being and her eternal destination. I concluded our conversation by hugging her and giving her a Bible written in her primary language, so she could continue reading other life-changing stories impacted by the merciful mission of Christ.

Would members from her household appreciate her newfound interest in biblical truth? Was it possible they would persecute her since this Truth stood in opposition to her family's embedded belief system? I prayed for the Lord to protect her and redeem her through the power of the Holy Spirit. One day, perhaps she, too, would boldly share the love and light of Jesus with His message of salvation. As we parted ways, I wondered what would come of that conversation with the unknown teenager. I left hopeful and thankful, though, since I knew that the God who saw and saved me when I was a young student was the same merciful Father who could transform this youth's life as well. **Psalm 139:16** states about the sovereign Creator, **"Your eyes saw me when I was formless; all my days were written in Your book and planned before a single one of them began."**

Did you know that the New Testament is filled with similar unplanned conversations about spiritual matters? Some involve an individual's dialogue with Jesus during His earthly ministry, but many other discussions describe or recount Jesus and His gospel message. These divinely-spurred chit-chats took place in various towns, different locations, among diverse groups, who were not necessarily familiar with each other, but nonetheless found a common interest. Moreover, some of the surprising dialogues recorded in the Bible occurred between individuals who were considered enemies, based on their generational upbringing.

One such spontaneous chat took place between Jesus and a nameless but known DIVORCED WOMAN BY THE WELL. It was an intentional conversation initiated by the Jewish Messiah with an unlikely Samaritan female; it began with His puzzling request for a drink of water, and concluded with her priceless realization that her encounter was with the Living Water. This life-changing exchange is another beneficial scriptural example of how numerous classes of people believed in Jesus, trusted His Word, and followed Him, which continues throughout our generation today.

Upon leaving Judea, Jesus with His disciples had deliberately traveled through the region of Samaria on their way to Galilee, even though other routes were available. In biblical times, Jews often avoided Samaria because of the deep-rooted, long-standing racial tension with the Samaritans. The town of Sychar, off the beaten path, was the precise location where Jesus met this unidentified woman at a local hotspot, the village's water supply, near property that the Hebrew Patriarch Jacob previously gave to his son Joseph.

As you may recognize in the scripture passage below, there were various reasons this unaccompanied woman was stunned by her bizarre encounter with this noticeably different stranger. A primary reason for her reaction was the prohibition against the socially inappropriate verbal exchange that began at the well; men did not typically speak with women in public settings, especially a Jewish male and a Samaritan female. For Jesus, however, this was just another day of ministry, but with an unparalleled opportunity to share His life-changing gospel message. The salvation of this unidentified woman's soul was at risk; that was more important to Jesus than social customs or a culture's opinion of Him.

Jesus did not dismiss divinely appointed moments to share the Good News of salvation with males and females, or Gentiles and Jews. On this occasion, He utilized a one-on-one conversation to engage in a mercy-filled dialogue with an unlikely half-breed. She understood the sting of being despised, rejected, and isolated by others; nonetheless, the merciful Messiah noticed and cared for this woman, as we read in **John 4:7-26**:

> [7] A woman of Samaria came to draw water. 'Give me a drink,' Jesus said to her, [8] because His disciples had gone into town to buy food. [9] 'How is it that You, a Jew, ask for a drink from me, a Samaritan woman?' she asked Him. For Jews do not associate with Samaritans. [10] Jesus answered, 'If you knew the gift of God, and Who is saying to you, "'Give me a drink,'" you would ask Him, and He would give you living water.' [11] 'Sir,' said the woman, 'You don't even have a bucket, and the well is deep. So where do You get this 'living water'? [12] You aren't greater than our father Jacob, are You? He gave us the well and drank from it himself, as did his sons and livestock.'
>
> [13] Jesus said, 'Everyone who drinks from this water will get thirsty again. [14] But whoever drinks from the water that I will give him will never get thirsty again. In fact, the water I will give him will become a well of water springing up in him for eternal life.' [15] 'Sir,' the woman said to Him, 'give me this water so that I won't get thirsty and come here to draw water.' [16] 'Go call your husband,' He told her, 'and come back here.' [17] 'I don't have a husband,' she answered. 'You have correctly said, "'I don't have a husband,'" Jesus said. [18] 'For you've had five husbands, and the man you now have is not your husband. What you have said is true.'
>
> [19] 'Sir,' the woman replied, 'I see that You are a Prophet. [20] Our ancestors worshiped on this mountain, but You

Jews say that the place to worship is in Jerusalem.' <sup>21</sup> Jesus told her, 'Believe me, woman, an hour is coming when you will worship the Father neither on this mountain nor in Jerusalem. <sup>22</sup> You Samaritans worship what you do not know. We worship what we know, because salvation is from the Jews. <sup>23</sup> But an hour is coming, and is now here, when the true worshipers will worship the Father in Spirit and in truth. Yes, the Father wants such people to worship Him. <sup>24</sup> God is Spirit, and those who worship Him must worship in Spirit and in truth.' <sup>25</sup> The woman said to Him, 'I know that the Messiah is coming (who is called Christ). When He comes, He will explain everything to us.' <sup>26</sup> Jesus told her, 'I, the One speaking to you, am He.'

In kicking off our study of six unidentified women who encountered one merciful Savior, we begin by looking at this biblical account that is most familiar to many who have studied the Bible. Since the unknown divorced woman's story recorded in John 4 follows the famous conversation between Jesus and a Jewish religious leader regarding spiritual rebirth (**John 3:1-21**), the story of this nameless Samaritan woman is taught from many pulpits. Her narrative makes a stark contrast between Jesus' privately held meeting at night with a respected Pharisee, versus openly talking about spiritual matters to a detested Samaritan in broad daylight. Jesus did not favor one or the other, since witnessing to both individuals was of paramount importance. Both were searching for something that was missing in their lives; each equally needed a Savior to satisfy their spiritual longing. The dialogue between Jesus and this unfamiliar woman was brief, but beneficial, without much delay in reaching the main point. It was fitting, however, that the physically worn-out Messiah started the conversation by talking about His need for a drink of water, since their meeting took place at Jacob's communal well.

It is helpful for us to observe a scene that depicts the humanity of the incarnate Jesus, with temporary bodily limitations, who got tired, thirsty, hungry, experienced physical pain, and so forth. It is a good reminder that He can sympathize with our weaknesses as humans, yet Christ remained without sin (**Hebrews 4:15**). The woman came alone to the well to draw water about the sixth hour of the day, when she saw Jesus sitting by Himself, perhaps caught off guard by His presence. It's significant that she did not join the typical timing of women traveling together to the community well to enjoy a leisurely chat with one another. This divorced woman was ostracized from the others; maintaining loyal female friendships proved difficult due to the nature of her current immoral living arrangements. Nevertheless, she was the unlikely prospect for salvation; the merciful Savior made the first critical move to stir up a brief but essential conversation with her. Her primary need flowed from her thirst for righteousness, and Jesus was the One who could satisfy that yearning by blessing her with His nonperishable provision (**Matthew 5:6**).

The vital encounter at the well between the Messiah and the nameless but known divorced woman demonstrates how Jesus addressed four common concerns facing individuals to direct on-the-spot conversations to the gospel message. As we explore these common concerns discussed by Jesus and the woman, notice how she assigned a different name to Him with the raising of each pressing issue: Jew, Sir, Prophet, and finally, Messiah the Christ. For each ascribed name, the personal nature strengthened, indicating that this curious lady gradually came to understand to Whom she was speaking—the renowned Savior of the world.

First, Jesus started the conversation by _pointing out the physical concern_. Both He and the woman sought water from the well because they were thirsty. Jesus had no bucket to get water from a deep well, but that was not the most startling aspect of this encounter. As previously referenced, the Samaritan female was curious why this male Jew was talking directly to her and asking for a kind favor, even though a woman could be directed by a man to draw water for him. Yet, who would she ask about this man? Who would be willing to answer her query? Furthermore, why was this Jewish man willing to share a well-used, communal bucket with her for a cup of water? She thought, *surely this unfamiliar stranger knows He is awkwardly crossing cultural boundaries in the name of a drink.* Was that worth it to Him? Yes, it was! According to **Isaiah 41:17**, the Lord God affirmed, **"The poor and the needy seek water, but there is none; their tongues are parched with thirst. I will answer them. I am the Lord, the God of Israel. I will not abandon them."**

Jesus set an example in this John 4 passage that demonstrated how a growing capacity for compassion begins with an awareness of another's pressing need beyond primarily focusing on your own interests, albeit important. **First Peter 3:8-9** exhorts the body of Christ to be, **"like-minded and sympathetic, love one another, and be compassionate and humble…giving a blessing, since you were called for this."** Jesus was aware of the woman's desperate need for a Savior; He also knew her openness to hearing the gospel message about the free gift of God for those willing to receive it. God's Son explained to the woman, **"If you knew the gift of God, and who is saying to you, 'Give me a drink,' you would ask Him, and He would give you living water" (John 4:10).**

Remarkably, Jesus took the necessary time, which was neither wasted nor in vain, to slowly shift this lady's basic knowledge *about* the Messiah to a genuine saving knowledge of the Christ. His compassionate, enduring patience supported continuing the conversation to arrive at the gospel message (**James 5:11**). She willingly listened and asked questions with interest, since she struggled to understand some of the concepts of spiritual matters Christ said. **Second Peter 3:9** reminds us that the Lord is patient with each one of us, not wanting anyone to perish, but wanting all to come to repentance by grace through faith in Jesus. Now, as was equally true and unfortunate then, many will continue to reject Christ and His gospel message, and decline His gift of salvation, but this should not impede a Christ-follower's efforts to faithfully share God's Word with others.

In writing about physical and spiritual concerns in his Gospel, John emphasizes the concepts of "life" throughout his biblical chapters. For example, he references new birth, bread of life, light of life, eternal life, and resurrected life—all pointing to the Son of God, Jesus. In this John 4 narrative, the notion of "living water" is explored, which intrigued the woman, and was a term used by Jesus to draw the woman into a deeper conversation that went beyond the physical necessity of drinking water because of excessive heat and thirst. This led to verbiage of Christ represented as the Living Water who offers a spiritual well springing up for eternal life to completely satisfy and refresh the thirsty soul (**Psalm 36:9**). **John 7:38-39** records this declaration from Jesus, **"If anyone is thirsty, let him come to Me and drink. The one who believes in Me, as the Scripture has said, will have streams of living water flow from deep within him."** These verses were a prophetic promise of the coming Holy Spirit who would dwell in the hearts of those that repented and believed in Jesus for eternal life.

After increasing the woman's interest when pointing out the physical concern, Jesus continued by *dealing with the ancestral concern*. This is where the woman questioned this unaccustomed, prohibited interaction between Samaritans and Jews. As previously stated, there was long-running racial tension between these two groups, who attempted to avoid each other at all costs. A Samaritan was born part Jew and part Gentile, a mixed race, and lacked sufficient proof of their original genealogy to determine if they were ancestrally connected to the chosen Hebrew nation.

Because they were not typically integrated into the worship practices of the Jewish community, Samaritans established their own temple and religious services within their designated region. They desired to be a part of the chosen family of God, but were not necessarily welcomed. The Hebrews excluded them, based on their heritage; that is, until Jesus stepped onto the scene. He began to tear apart the misconstrued notion that salvation was only for the Jews (**Romans 3:29**), even though salvation originated from the Jews in the person of Jesus Christ (**John 4:22**). His gospel message was an invitation to anyone who listened to the truth, repented of their sin, trusted Jesus for salvation, believed His Word, and followed Him, regardless of their gender, race, or family ancestry (**Ephesians 2:12-14**).

The nameless woman knew bits and pieces of the Hebrew lineage, thus regarding Jacob as one of the greatest patriarchs descended from the house of Israel. He was her point of reference as an impressive ancestral leader, who kindly provided for his people, which included her tribe. She wanted to know if this unfamiliar Jewish man sitting at Jacob's well was just as supreme in supplying a mysterious outlet for obtaining water. How could Jesus offer *better* water than Jacob, that others, including outsiders, had enjoyed over generations? Where would this unusual stranger acquire this "living water"? Moreover, why would Jesus offer it to her? The woman's initial craving for this seemingly magical water was a matter of convenience to her, to permanently quench her thirst and provide a way for her to avoid returning to the well. That vital errand not only involved hard work, but also heightened her awareness of being an easy target for another's gossip or their hurtful contempt. This was precisely the moment when Jesus addressed the next concern.

Upon pointing out the physical concern, then dealing with the ancestral concern, Jesus next *brought up the personal concern*. I appreciate the subtle but straightforward manner in which Jesus initiated the issue regarding personal sin for this five-time divorced woman, who had jumped into another unhealthy relationship with a sixth man. We don't know the reason for all the failed marriage relationships. Perhaps she was searching for a human relationship to fully satisfy her, only to experience recurring disappointment when the union fell short of her expectations. Or maybe she struggled with her identity related to her mixed ethnic background, not knowing where she belonged or to whom she was connected, seeking a permanent place to fit in. As a divorced woman from a 1st Century generation, she would have been marked as a repeat participant in infidelity, and referred to as a defiled adulteress, possibly shunned for her blatant unfaithfulness to a marriage agreement (**Matthew 5:31-32**).

This nameless but known woman needed a new perspective on the original biblical mandate of the marriage covenant, one man-one woman-one lifetime for the glory of God. Mankind's sinful rebellion against the commands of God impacted this sacred matrimonial covenant resulting in bitter struggles between spouses throughout generations. A forsaken divorced woman was surely ready to embrace the divine devotion of a faithful heavenly husband, who would neither leave her, nor forsake her, as described by God through the prophet in **Isaiah 54:5-6; "Indeed, your Husband is your Maker – His name is the Lord of Armies – and the Holy One of Israel is your Redeemer; He is called the God of the whole earth. For the Lord has called you, like a wife deserted and wounded in spirit, a wife of one's youth when she is rejected."**

Though divorce was permitted in biblical times because of human hard-heartedness and faithlessness to the marriage union, this was neither the ideal for a household, nor God's design for marriage (**Malachi 2:15-16; Matthew 19:3-9**). Thankfully, God has made a way for a righteous and permanent union between the heavenly Bridegroom and His redeemed church bride, a household consisting of godly offspring through the finished redemptive work of Jesus on behalf of His spiritual family (**Revelation 21:2-3, 6**). God's purposeful plans are not frustrated by humanity's moral failure. You and I cannot, however, appreciate the matchless mercy of the gospel message of salvation, the good news of forgiveness, restoration, and eternal life in Christ, without first addressing the bad news about ourselves—deeply depraved people in need of a Savior. We must deal with the serious matter of unconfessed sin and blatant transgression of God's law.

Jesus smoothly but directly referred to this personal concern by advising the woman to go call her husband and bring him before Jesus. It is evident that she recognized the truth of the situation within that moment, but only gave a short reply when confronted with the reality of her sin. She most likely was aware she could not solve the undeniable issue by her own methods. She needed someone greater than Israel's forefather, Jacob; she needed the coming Savior. Thankfully for her sake, the anticipated Messiah was sitting right in front of her, prompting this verbal exchange about spiritual matters and offering her an invaluable, eternal solution.

Repentance is necessary through spiritual conviction before genuine faith can take root and grow through the hearing and living of the Word of God. Repentance is more than confessing your wrongdoing by agreeing with God that you have sinned against Him and His commands; it is deliberately turning away from sinful actions to place your trust in Jesus and follow Him and His Word. This is a change in your heart, mind, attitude, and priorities when you align them with God's Word. Conviction of sin, a necessary work of the Holy Spirit, prepares the heart to receive the gospel message by faith, to encourage you to humbly surrender to God, and admit there is a sin problem that is separating you from engaging in a personal relationship with Christ. **Proverbs 28:13** explains, **"The one who conceals his sins will not prosper, but whoever confesses and renounces them will find mercy."** Authentic sin confession leads to genuine spiritual conversion for the glory of God and the good of the regenerated child of God (**1 John 1:9**).

When Jesus called out the woman's sin, making her suspiciously aware that He was familiar with her hidden iniquities, she attempted to change the subject and distract this obvious prophet from continuing an uncomfortably personal conversation. Jesus was righteously prying into her private affairs, not to condemn her, but to deliver her, and bring her to a stark realization of her desperate need for a merciful Savior and His salvation. The holy, blameless Messiah, who had the ability to know the disgraceful, unclean parts of her life, graciously desired to purify her so she could share in unadulterated fellowship with the Lord. Jesus was mindful of this woman's potential and purpose for the glory of God to be an extraordinary witness for Christ upon her redemption by faith, yet the personal sin issue needed to be addressed. Because of the timely transforming work of Christ, what was developing within the Samaritan woman was a zeal to proclaim a verbal testimony, impacting an entire village of Samaritans, about her changed life affected by the matchless mercy of God.

Jesus did not shy away from the discourse when the woman brought up other somewhat insignificant religious items, for example, discussing the locations for a worship service. Instead, He gently redirected the dialogue to emphasize the importance of worshiping and serving the One True Living God. Christ accomplished this by patiently explaining the difference between a true worshiper serving the Lord in Spirit and truth, versus a false one who followed basic tradition, but in whom no spiritual heart change existed.

After Jesus rightly addressed the unidentified divorced woman's *physical, ancestral, and personal concerns*, their conversation wrapped up by reaching the core of the talk: Jesus <u>*focused the discussion on the spiritual concern*</u>.

Arriving at a popular community well, an ordinary Samaritan woman, who had probably spent years feeling isolated and trapped in her spiritual poverty, always searching for lasting satisfaction, yet plagued by discontentment, was unexpectedly welcomed into the family of God, though that welcome was unmerited. She could rejoice in the Lord for His love and mercy, as declared in **John 7:17, "You gave me life and faithful love, and Your care has guarded my life."**

Her biblical story highlights how a nameless but known individual who, banned from religious inclusion by her sinful past, was secured for her eternal future in God's kingdom through salvation in Jesus. A simple discussion that began with questions about water, turned into inquiries of wonder, progressed with conviction of wrongdoing, developed into an understanding about worship, and concluded with the truth of the Word. Because of this merciful meeting by means of a spontaneous conversation, the compassionate and caring Savior forever changed this seemingly forgotten woman's life. Her brief encounter further impacted an entire community to follow and fellowship with Jesus. **"For the Lord your God is gracious and merciful; He will not turn His face away from you if you return to Him" (2 Chronicles 30:9).**

The woman initially struggled with her understanding of absolute truth in the person of Jesus through the written Word of God; yet she proclaimed the one spiritual truth she was certain of, that the Messiah, known as the Christ, was coming soon **(John 4:25)**. Her simple admission of faith hinted at her hopeful confidence that the Messiah was coming on her behalf also, regardless of others treating her as a shunned Samaritan. Even if this officially defiled, but now mercifully delivered woman didn't quite know what the prophesied coming of the future Messiah entailed, she was waiting with optimistic anticipation of Christ, looking forward to the long-awaited Anointed One explaining everything to her and those in her community.

Perhaps the Sychar residents were primed and ready to have their existence make sense amid a harsh society where they felt unloved and discarded, and left them wondering about their purpose. What did they hope the sacred Messiah would explain? What answers were they searching for? How did they believe the Christ would make a difference for them? We do not know for sure the answers to these questions, but what we can deduce is that upon the unnamed woman's profession of faith in Christ, Jesus revealed His identity as the genuine Messiah—the One who was speaking to her. He cared enough to take the road less traveled, not veering away from a despised town, to share the marvelous mercy of God with a known hurting individual, and to change her life forever. Remarkably, the risen Savior's final commission to His disciples prior to His Ascension, included His continuing care for the region of Samaria, as recorded in **Acts 1:8, "You will receive power when the Holy Spirit has come on you, and you will be My witnesses in Jerusalem, in all Judea and Samaria, and to the ends of the earth."**

How did this transformed Samaritan woman respond when she learned she had been in the presence of Jesus, the Son of God? **John 4:28-30** provides the exciting answer, **"Then the woman left her water jar, went into town, and told the people, 'Come, see a man who told me everything I ever did. Could this be the Messiah?' They left the town and made their way to Him."** The unnamed divorced woman, personally changed by the matchless mercy of God, had an immediate concern for those who resided in her town, whether they believed her testimony or not. She left the water jar behind, since the physical need was outweighed by the spiritual need. She recognized that the Messiah Himself had met her primary need for a Savior. This grateful converted woman was motivated to immediately tell others about Jesus, to invite them to come meet Him for themselves, and to urge them to listen to His life-changing gospel message. How remarkable that the townsfolk did not turn on her, but ran instead to meet Jesus. They desired to hear His sermon of salvation, too, yearning to spend more time in His presence, which led them to placing their faith in Him as Savior (**John 4:39-42**). What do you suppose the crowd asked the woman afterwards? Perhaps, "Hey, what's your name?" However, the Son of God already knew her name and did not need that detail within their memorable conversation.

**First John 1:1-3** speaks of the Word of Life, **"That life was revealed, and we have seen it and we testify and declare to you the eternal life that was with the Father and was revealed to us – what we have seen and heard we also declare to you, so that you may also have fellowship with us; and indeed our fellowship is with the Father and with His Son, Jesus Christ."**

A secluded Samaritan woman was not forgotten by God; neither was her neighborhood. Her inclusion within the redeemed, unified, spiritual family of combined Jews and Gentiles reflected God's undeserved kindness graciously extended to an unlikely individual. Just think, it all started with Jesus' impromptu dialogue with a nameless but known divorced woman by a well. Though Christ knew the truth about her sordid past, He cared more about her eternal future, and freely forgave her, spiritually restoring her to a right relationship with God. Her encounter with the true Messiah might have disrupted her original plans, but radically changed her life's direction moving forward. In **Isaiah 52:6-7**, the Lord God declares, **"My people will know My Name; therefore they will know on that day that I am He who says, 'Here I am.' How beautiful on the mountains are the feet of the herald, who proclaims peace, who brings news of good things, who proclaims salvation."**

Only Christ has the power to heal the wounds a brokenhearted woman suffered from multiple failed relationships, and to call her to a purposeful mission that shifted her priorities to boldly proclaiming the name of Jesus to others. Hers was the testimonial of what an old, condemned life is like before meeting Christ—being sentenced to death by sin— and what the new, redeemed life is like after encountering Christ—the promise of eternal life. The prophesied Messiah, who values people from all nations and tribes, indeed had come to spiritually satisfy thirsty sinners in need of living water. Pastor and author Chuck Swindoll offers this encouragement: "There is no one you will ever meet, no friend you will ever make, who can do for you what Jesus can do. No one else can change your inner heart. No one else can turn your entire life around. No one else can remove not only your sins but the guilt and shame that are part of that whole ugly package."[5]

Perhaps you are facing some of the same common concerns Jesus addressed within John 4, whether you are a follower of Christ or not. Yet the ultimate solution to the issues you might be confronting, whether physical, ancestral, personal, or spiritual, is the person of Jesus Christ. He is the holy Anointed One who came, lived, died, and resurrected to provide the gift of salvation by grace through faith, granting forgiveness of sins, and promising eternal life. Your challenging concerns are the perfect opportunity to come near to Christ and drink from His refreshing well, to listen to His nourishing gospel message, and believe His timeless Word. Jesus loves and cares about you and desires to share in a personal relationship with you. Genuine peace and lasting satisfaction can be found only in Jesus Christ. **"Choose life so that you and your descendants may live, love the Lord your God, obey Him, and remain faithful to Him. For He is your life" (Deuteronomy 30:19-20).**

---

[5] Charles R. Swindoll, *Life is 10% What Happens to You and 90% How You React* (Nelson Books: Nashville, TN, 2023), 60.

**Application Acrostic**

**L**isten to Jesus' message

**I**nvite others to believe in Jesus

**F**ollow Jesus as your Source for life

**E**njoy fellowship with Jesus

**Thinking Through This**

- Consider the last time you engaged in an impromptu conversation with someone about spiritual matters. What did you discuss and what was the outcome?
- Which of the four common concerns (physical, ancestral, personal, spiritual) described above are you struggling with in your current circumstances?
- If there is a person or group you avoid because of past issues or recurring frustrations, how might you alter your outlook to be burdened for them rather than remain bothered by them?
- What may be impeding you from growing spiritually in a deeper relationship with Jesus?

**Further Findings of God's Mercy**

Read **Luke 10:25-37** to study the parable of a *nameless but known* Samaritan traveler journeying down a familiar road.

# Chapter 3

## THE ADULTEROUS WOMAN AT THE CENTER

*Judgment is God's justice confronting moral inequity,
whereas mercy is God's goodness confronting human guilt and suffering.*

In August 1993, shortly after my spiritual conversion at the age of 21, I got involved in a local church and participated in their singles ministry. I joined their co-ed softball team and felt drawn to contribute to the team. As the season progressed, and since I could run fast, I was strategically placed in the batting lineup to get a hit, get on base, and be prepared to score. I found the camaraderie exciting and the crowd's applause intoxicating, yet the harmful arrogance mounting within my heart blinded me. Naïvely unaware, I was poised to learn a painful but necessary lesson regarding that pride that inevitably comes before the fall.

The momentous game day left me with physical scars and a new perspective on compassion in action. As I recall, I had a single 1st base hit and was set to run to 2nd, mindful that the teammate after me was a homerun hitter. He also was a swift runner, which meant I had to kick it into gear to stay ahead of him when rounding the bases. As expected, he hit the ball hard, and it soared to the outfield near the fence; the opponents scampered to snag the ball and throw it home. As I watched the trajectory of the batted ball, I took off running to 2nd base, rounded the corner, and looked ahead while making my way to 3rd base. Since I could no longer see what was happening in the outfield, I relied on the 3rd base coach, who directed me to run to home plate. Meanwhile, I could hear the crowd cheering from the bleachers along with my teammate's hurried command behind me, "Go! Go! Go!" Unfortunately, the burden of scoring and the added pressure from my fellow player worked against me.

I was half-way home with my eyes fixed on the opposing catcher, who was positioned by home plate to receive the thrown ball and tag me out, when my legs buckled, and I started falling. Knowing I was going down, I quickly deduced that I had a fighting chance to successfully reach the plate, so I stretched out my arms and hands as far as I could and attempted to use the forward momentum to my advantage by sliding headfirst into homebase.

My headfirst approach did not go as planned. When the dust settled and the crowd fell silent in anticipation of the outcome, clearly I had fallen short about a foot from the plate. I was stretched out flat on my stomach with a face-plant in the dirt. The opposing team's catcher came up to me with ball in hand, reached down, and gently tagged me before declaring, "You're out!" The overlapping result meant no homerun for the teammate behind me, since he was held back at 3rd base.

To say I was a letdown to my team is one thing, but since this was a public occurrence, I felt like a humiliated failure. Some of the spectators laughed, while others expressed disappointment at a missed score. Some onlookers probably thought I deliberately face-planted as a strange, unsuccessful strategy. No one could have known I mistakenly face-planted because I fell and was trying to keep moving to score. Had that been the end of the story, I likely would have quit the team. However, the difference was the timely mercy shown to me in that embarrassing moment. The least likely person on the field chose to offer kindness instead of condemnation.

The competing team's catcher, who had the right to tag me out, was not dismissive of the rules of the game, but he graciously used the opportunity to show concern for my well-being. Without further verbal judgment, he extended his hand out to me to help me up off the ground. He dusted me off without laughing at me, and then quietly inquired if I was okay. This sympathetic catcher's calm demeanor outweighed all the harsh reactions to the play.

I felt alone and disgraced as I stood before the spectators with fresh wounds to both my skin and ego from the fall, but oddly, an unfamiliar sense of peace washed over me as I looked into the catcher's tender eyes and heard his gentle voice. I was surprised that a stranger offered more compassion to me in a horrific personal moment than my friends in the dugout who knew me prior to my downfall. I did not anticipate my predicament, nor could I change the outcome, yet I could choose how to respond to this mortifying occurrence that moment. Would I have a renewed outlook on God's mercy, since I was impacted by an outsider's compassion encouraging me when I was down in the dirt?

This is the question possibly pondered by a biblical nameless but known ADULTEROUS WOMAN AT THE CENTER one shameful, but momentous day, when she unexpectedly encountered Jesus. Her story is found in **John 8:2-11**.

> ²**At dawn He went to the temple again, and all the people were coming to Him. He sat down and began to teach them.** ³**Then the scribes and the Pharisees brought a woman caught in adultery, making her stand in the center.** ⁴**'Teacher,' they said to Him, 'this woman was caught in the act of committing adultery.** ⁵**In the law Moses commanded us to stone such women. So what do You say?'** ⁶**They asked this to trap Him, in order that they might have evidence to accuse Him. Jesus stooped down**

and started writing on the ground with His finger. ⁷When they persisted in questioning Him, He stood up and said to them, 'The one without sin among you should be the first to throw a stone at her.' ⁸Then He stooped down again and continued writing on the ground. ⁹When they heard this, they left one by one, starting with the older men. Only He was left, with the woman in the center. ¹⁰When Jesus stood up, He said to her, 'Woman, where are they? Has no one condemned you?' ¹¹'No one, Lord,' she answered. 'Neither do I condemn you,' said Jesus. 'Go, and from now on do not sin anymore.'

It is necessary for me to insert a brief disclaimer regarding the adulterous woman's story. Some question the validity and placement of this Scripture passage, as recorded in the Gospel of John. It is a matter of an editorial debatable question by contextual critics on whether this historical event was included in the book of John in the earliest New Testament manuscripts, or placed elsewhere in the Bible, or not included at all. But there is no heretical doctrine within this John 8 text. The content of the encounter is consistent with the character of Jesus and shows a relevant moment during His earthly ministry. This biblical account demonstrates a remarkable example of Jesus extending mercy to an undeserving, but grateful individual, and provides treasured takeaways; therefore, I have chosen to include this unnamed woman's story within my *Nameless but Known* book. Regardless of your stance on this matter, it does not change the fact that the New Testament remains completely reliable and trustworthy.

Similar to the other unnamed women discussed in this book, the story of the adulterous woman at the center spurs each of us to consider what we would do if placed in a comparable uncomfortable situation, particularly if it happened during a religious gathering with a preacher delivering a sermon. How would you react as a bystander in the crowd hearing this allegation? How would you respond if you were the humiliated woman standing in the middle of the eyewitnesses? What would you do or say if your most shocking secret offense was suddenly made public? What if you were the accuser of another, but the preacher then confronted you about your own hidden transgressions before a verdict was rendered for the alleged offender?

The accusation about the woman was not just hearsay, since the scriptural text defines the proof as her being caught in the act of committing adultery before she was brought before Jesus. As we study this story of God's matchless mercy to an adulterous woman, it is not only the graciousness of the divine Christ we find, but also the grotesqueness of depraved humanity.

By chapter 8 in the book of John, the brief earthly ministry of Jesus is well-underway. Many had believed in His message and mission by faith and chose to follow Him, but others had deserted Him because His message was too tough to accept. Because of Jesus, the crowd was often divided, not always knowing what to think of this unusual God-Man, who was drawn to the marginalized, and had the power to heal, and authority to forgive sin. Still others had become suspicious of Him and were intimidated by Him, particularly the religious leaders who included the scribes and Pharisees. Over time, they exhibited toxic hypocrisy and dangerous hatred toward the Messiah in their relentless pursuit to dismantle His ministry, tarnish His reputation, undermine His redemptive message of salvation, and expose Him as a liar and a fraud, though all their attempts were unsuccessful.

Since Jesus regularly taught in the temple, the Pharisees repeatedly interrupted His gospel-driven message with their misguided agenda. They consistently sought to seize Him, find a loophole to trap Him in His words, or trick Him into breaking the Mosaic Law. The local religious sect relished questioning the creditability of Jesus as a well-known teacher. Without rejecting the Law of Moses, He had since gained a reputation for compassion and forgiveness among the predominately Jewish society. Nevertheless, the tense scene in John 8 is no different from other scenes that displayed the cunning antics of a self-righteous bunch, whose objective was to take down the Son of God at the expense of a terrified female trapped like a pawn in the middle of their scheme.

Within this study of a nameless but known adulterous woman standing at the center, Jesus makes three declarations in response to the allegation against her. This does not signify that discipline, punishment, or consequences should not be natural components of wrongdoing. God's Law benefits society, since all governing authorities are subject to God as His instituted servants (**Romans 13:1-7**). In Jesus' first declaration, He rendered a _challenge_: **"The one without sin among you should be the first to throw a stone at her" (John 8:7)**.

Before Jesus offered this challenge to the woman's accusers, the Pharisees announced the indictment against her. Committing adultery was forbidden by Hebrew Law and warranted a legal penalty, as long as 2-3 valid witnesses could testify to the crime allegedly committed (**Deuteronomy 19:15**). The Law of Moses was sufficient to accuse the Hebrew people of sin, but the Law could neither justify nor cleanse them from their unrighteousness (**Romans 3:19-24**). Ironically, the religious officials boasted of knowing and upholding the Levitical Law, while questioning whether the so-called Messianic prophet was familiar with the same Old Testament commandments. They faltered in following the Hebrew statutes while showing their ignorance of the written decrees (**John 7:19**). According to the Law, _both_ guilty persons who engaged in an adulterous affair were to be brought before the religious court, confronted with their wrongdoing, and issued the consequences for their disobedience _together_ (**Leviticus 20:10**). In this case, only the alleged adulteress was dragged before Jesus without any reference to the male adulterer.

The Bible does not clarify if this alleged act of adultery was a one-time offense or a habitual practice. Neither do we know if the accused woman was married, thus committing adultery with a man who was not her husband, or conversely, single and engaging in an illicit affair with a married man. What is clear is that an act of infidelity took place, thus negatively impacting two different households. The original Ten Commandments given by God to His chosen people spoke against the sin of adultery in **Exodus 20:14**, but Jesus expounded on this commandment in **Matthew 5:27-28** during His Sermon on the Mount. He spoke frankly into the heart of the matter of adultery: **"You have heard that it was said, 'Do not commit adultery.' But I tell you, everyone who looks at a woman lustfully has already committed adultery with her in his heart."**

The temptation of adultery begins with lust in the heart before reaching a defilement of the marriage bed, however, **1 Corinthians 10:13** reminds us that even though temptation is common to mankind residing in a fallen world, God is faithful to not allow you and me to be tempted beyond what we are able to endure. He provides a way of escape, a pathway out of temptation, IF we will make the deliberate choice to follow that way out. Furthermore, **Galatians 6:1** urges healthy accountability among a committed body of believers who care for one another's well-being: **"Brothers and sisters, if someone is overtaken in any wrongdoing, you who are spiritual, restore such a person with a gentle spirit, watching out for yourselves so that you also won't be tempted."**

Even when an accusation is accurate, we can be mistaken in our method of approaching the individual to address the offense. Restoration of the spiritual brother or sister should be the goal that includes a gentle spirit speaking the truth in love (**Ephesians 4:15**).

It is peculiar that the Pharisees asked Jesus, **"So, what do You say?"** once they finished pronouncing the indictment against the woman standing in the center of the crowd. Up to that point, Jesus had done most of the talking in His teaching during the temple gathering; the religious leaders just needed to listen to His Words. They asked their question to aid them in bringing an accusation against Jesus Himself, however, it stands as a crucial question for each of us to ask the Savior. To rightly discover what Jesus has or has not said about a particular matter, we must regularly read and study God's written Word, the Bible.

If the accusers were truly interested in Jesus' opinion, then all they needed to do was listen and learn and be ready to put into practice Christ's instructions, such as His guidance for restoring a brother or sister who had sinned against them. In **Matthew 18:15-17**, Jesus taught, **"If your brother sins against you, go tell him his fault between you and him alone. If he listens to you, you have won your brother. But if he won't listen, take one or two others with you, so that by the testimony of two or three witnesses every fact may be established. If he doesn't pay attention to them, tell the church."** Privately confronting sin as the first step, especially among a God-fearing body of believers, can be a beneficial process for the guilty party. This provides them with a chance to listen and a choice to make things right; but then offers the opportunity for the confronter to come alongside the alleged guilty one and wisely guide him or her in their next steps. Had the religious faultfinders chosen this divinely orchestrated reconciliation strategy in confronting both adulterer and adulteress to urge them to: 1) repent, 2) turn from their sin, 3) believe God's Word, and 4) follow Jesus, then perhaps the religious leaders' initial fault-finding motives would have been short lived; a broken marriage could have been restored.

Shortly after Jesus delivered this Matthew 18 message, His close disciple, Peter, approached Him and asked, **"Lord, how many times must I forgive my brother or sister who sins against me? As many as seven times?"** To which Jesus answered, **"I tell you, not as many as seven, but seventy times seven" (Matthew 18:21-22)**. Forgiven people forgive other people and Christ-followers are forgiven people. This is not to suggest that you repeatedly subject yourself to harmful and dangerous abuse in the *milieu* of forgiveness. The Lord's lovingkindness can provide support and prompt genuine forgiveness from the injured party and heal him or her from the harmful, lasting effects of bitterness and unforgiveness. I'm grateful that God's matchless mercy changes lives, impacts circumstances, and grants wisdom for challenging choices.

In his book, *Seeing and Savoring Jesus Christ*©, pastor and author John Piper writes, "Justice is essential among the perfections of God's glory. But mercy is paramount...if justice can be preserved, it is the apex of glory to show mercy. For this reason Jesus Christ came into the world."[6]

Numerous Bible scholars have attempted to discern what Jesus was indicating through His temporary silence and obscure finger-writing in the dirt after the demanding accusers presented the criminal charge against the disgraced woman. We can only speculate though; perhaps the Messiah paused to give those present the chance to think through the weightiness of the public accusation or the seriousness of their own hidden sins. Maybe the omniscient Son of God was writing the undisclosed offenses of those seeking condemnation against the woman. Regardless of the unspecified reason, the hushed crowd and

---

[6] John Piper, *Seeing and Savoring Jesus Christ* (Wheaton, IL: Crossway, 2004), 84-85.

silent Savior did not remain in this subdued position for long, since the woman's adversaries persisted in questioning Jesus rather than further interrogating the offender in their center.

Did you notice in the John 8 passage that the transgressions of the accusers were not made public within this setting? Their turning and walking away in response to Jesus' charge that the one without sin had permission to throw a stone spoke volumes and tacitly confirmed their guilt of prior sins. Jesus did not deny the accuracy of the Law, nor dismiss the woman's alleged transgression. Rather, Jesus challenged the leaders to contemplate their own sin in light of God's mercy. In **Daniel 9:8-9,** the prophet prayed, **"Lord, public shame belongs to us...because we have sinned against You. Compassion and forgiveness belong to the Lord our God, though we have rebelled against Him."**

Everyone in that moment stood guilty of transgressions, except ONE, the sinless Son of God, who did not pick up a stone to throw at a single, sinful individual among the group, even though He alone had that right. His earthly mission had been pre-determined by His heavenly Father, which included the substitutionary public sacrifice of shedding His blood on a cross for the forgiveness of sin. Christ's urgent, but compassionate message remained the same, whether addressing a prideful accuser or an ashamed adulteress. He called sinners to repent with an invitation to trust and follow Him. The woman's isolated sin appeared greater to those prosecuting her, but Christ's mercy shone greater still in His response to the accusers and His reaction to the adulteress.

After Jesus challenged the woman's accusers, in His second declaration, Jesus spoke to the condemned woman and offered *charity*: **"Woman, where are they? Has no one condemned you?...Neither do I condemn you" (John 8:10-11).**

Like most of the other unidentified women in *Nameless but Known*, we have minimal details of the story of this unspecified female. We may have questions such as: What drove her into the arms of a man who was not her husband, especially with extreme consequences attached to such a risky move? Did she ignore the warning signs along the way? What might the parties have done differently to prevent this act of unfaithfulness? To aid future decisions, it is beneficial to learn from another's mistakes, your prior experiences, and even personal mishaps, but aren't you grateful, like I am, that God's mercy is frequently displayed by a charitable advocate within an individual's harrowing moment?

Jesus did not question the accused woman if she had recently acted immorally, since He is all-knowing of all things for every person (**John 2:24-25**). Plus, the woman on trial never denied her wrongdoing, nor blamed another person, nor attempted to further cover up her offense. She barely said a word. Rather, Jesus questioned her accusers in connection with their premeditated plan to condemn her to death through public stoning, while principally seeking to discredit Christ's mission. Alas, no individual within the crowd was further judged that day because of the kindness of the majestic Messiah.

Perhaps you understand what it's like to bear shameful scars linked to unwise decisions, but those former wounds are no match for the merciful Redeemer, who can restore a person's dignity by faith in Christ, even after public failure. **Romans 10:10-11** explains, **"One believes with the heart, resulting in righteousness, and one confesses with the mouth, resulting in salvation. For the Scripture says, Everyone who believes on Him will not be put to shame."**

When envisioning this moment of surprising charity the divine Advocate offered to an undeserving lawbreaker, I wonder if the adulteress, aware that all eyes were on her, stood with her head bowed, her eyes closed, and her arms wrapped around herself in a feeble attempt to hide her public shame? Perhaps the solitary woman standing in the center of the crowd, waiting to be hit with the first thrown stone, deeply felt what the Psalmist described in **Psalm 142:3b-5a, "Along this path I travel they have hidden a trap for me. Look to the right and see: no one stands up for me; there is no refuge for me; no one cares about me. I cry to you, Lord."** As Jesus stood up to speak to the adulteress after her challenged, disgruntled opponents walked away, did this spared lady timidly lift up her head to gaze into the eyes of the compassionate Savior before verbalizing her short reply to His question, **"Woman…has no one condemned you"**?

Utilizing just a few words to answer Christ's question, **"No one, Lord,"** the acquitted woman acknowledged Jesus as Lord, who saved her from death. She was not given the opportunity to plead her case when placed on trial, but this unforeseen Advocate stepped in. He wisely and kindly intervened on her behalf, thus providing a second chance for a new life. Similarly, in **Romans 8:34**, the Apostle Paul asked a direct question followed by a clear answer, **"Who is the one who condemns? Christ Jesus is the One who died, but even more, has been raised; He also is at the right hand of God and intercedes for us."** What did this pardoned woman do with her newfound life reinstated by the charitable Christ? We don't have an answer, since the Scripture is not explicit, but what would you have done after realizing that you were granted charity in place of condemnation?

Prior to the public scene referenced in our John 8 text, Jesus had met privately with a Pharisee named Nicodemus to discuss matters of spiritual rebirth and the kingdom of God. An expert in the Law and a Jewish ruler, Nicodemus had some questions for this peculiar Rabbi, who used the occasion to proclaim the Good News of salvation to him recorded in **John 3:16-18: "For God loved the world in this way: He gave His one and only Son, so that everyone who believes in Him**

will not perish but have eternal life. For God did not send His Son into the world to condemn the world, but to save the world through Him. Anyone who believes in Him is not condemned, but anyone who does not believe is already condemned because he has not believed in the name of the one and only Son of God."

Condemnation is not merely linked to sinful choices, but is always connected to unbelief in Christ. For one who stands before the Father, condemned guilty of sin, only God's Son is able to extend merciful charity by the gift of salvation by grace through faith in Him.

Jesus, the innocent Son of God, faced a religious tribunal Himself, falsely accused of blasphemy, required to participate in an unlawful trial, subsequently condemned to death, cruelly mocked by the multitude, and tortured by tyrannical soldiers. Afterward, He was nailed to a cross to die an excruciatingly painful public death, shedding His righteous blood for the forgiveness of sins. From the cross, during His worst hour of suffering in paying the penalty owed by all others, the divine Advocate prayed to His heavenly Father and included this petition: **"Father, forgive them, because they do not know what they are doing" (Luke 23:33-34)**.

The encounter presented in our John 8 passage between a merciful Advocate confronting an adversary on behalf of an adulteress provides a fascinating depiction of the battle between death versus life. One group sought condemnation for the offender, versus one Savior who showed unanticipated compassion toward the lawbreaker. The accusers ordered the due penalty for sin, while the Redeemer offered mercy instead, aware He was to pay the ultimate price on the cross for sinful mankind. **Romans 8:1-4** offers a proclamation of hope, **"Therefore, there is now no condemnation for those in Christ Jesus, because the law of the Spirit of life in Christ Jesus has set you free from the law of sin and death. For what the law could not do since it was weakened by the flesh, God did. He condemned sin in the flesh by sending His own Son in the**

**likeness of sinful flesh as a sin offering, in order that the law's requirement would be fulfilled in us who do not walk according to the flesh but according to the Spirit."**

Following His challenge to the accusers, and offering charity to the adulteress, in Jesus' third and final declaration, He issued a *charge*: **"Go, and from now on do not sin anymore" (John 8:11).**

A day of deserved death reversed into a day of spared life, with a follow-up charge to an adulteress, and those in earshot, to choose life in Christ by turning away from past sin. The Bible proclaims victory in the risen Messiah in **Colossians 2:13-15: "And when you were dead in your trespasses and in the uncircumcision of your flesh, He made you alive with Him and forgave us all our trespasses. He erased the certificate of debt, with its obligations, that was against us and opposed to us, and has taken it away by nailing it to the cross. He disarmed the rulers and authorities and disgraced them publicly; He triumphed over them in Him."**

When a wrongdoer is caught in sin and called out, their initial reaction may be denial, or an excuse, or blame, or remorse, but what the sinner needs most is repentance. Remorse is a typical reaction that flows from a guilty person who seeks mercy from selfish motives because they are sorry they got caught and are subjected to painful consequences. They may temporarily regret their wrongdoing, but they are not necessarily motivated to alter their sinful course by living differently. Mercy recognizes remorse, but fosters repentance, which makes the greater difference.

Repentance expresses itself in genuine sorrow for wrongdoing by which the guilty party is inclined to change their destructive habits for the better because of their penitent heart. They have an honest shift in their mindset, by the working of the Holy Spirit, to acknowledge their misconduct, turn from their sin, and choose a different course of behavior through faith in Christ. The repentant seeks to benefit rather than harm themself or another person. They humbly accept and appreciate Christ's mercy, since Jesus changes a sinner's life for eternity. (Refer to **Luke 23:32-43** to read of a grueling, yet magnificent moment of a repentant criminal eternally impacted by the Messiah's mercy.)

The nameless woman's life was valuable in the sight of Jesus, even though she had fallen short of God's holy standard (**Romans 3:23**). With His charge to the adulteress to go and sin no more, Jesus offered her a second chance, and a personal choice to leave her life of willful sinning and choose to live for God's glory aligned with the truth of God's Word. Jesus' biological half-brother, James, exhorted a similar charge to a body of believers in **James 5:19-20, "My brothers and sisters, if any among you strays from the truth, and someone turns him back, let that person know that whoever turns a sinner from the error of his way will save his soul from death and cover a multitude of sins."** Only Jesus knows the potential of a redeemed person who has been changed by the sanctifying mercy of God. As they make the challenging choice to abstain from sinful practices and faithfully follow Jesus by believing His Word and relying on the indwelling power of the Holy Spirit, the Lord will utilize that person in a mighty way for His divine purpose to further impact God's kingdom (**1 Corinthians 6:9-11**).

A desire and decision to refrain from habitual sinful practices begins with a humble prayer of repentance to the Lord, acknowledging your need for Jesus and His Word to break free from slavery to sin. In **Psalm 19:12-13**, the servant pleads to God, **"Who perceives his unintentional sins? Cleanse me from my hidden faults. Moreover, keep your servant from willful sins; do not let them rule me. Then I will be blameless and cleansed from blatant rebellion."** We also need to extend grace to ourselves and others when a desire for faithfulness is overcome by the craving of temptation. This further calls for surrender, mercy, prayer, support, and humbly returning to the lovingkindness of our Savior. The writer of **Psalm 40:11-13** understood this inherent struggle and prayed, **"Lord, You do not withhold Your compassion from me. Your constant love and truth will always guard me. For troubles without number have surrounded me; my iniquities have overtaken me; I am unable to see…Lord, be pleased to rescue me; hurry to help me, Lord."**

Separated from Jesus and His redeeming blood for forgiveness of sins, every human being remains culpable for their sin, condemned to death, and subject to the penalty of the wrath of God. The corrupt nature of mankind is sin, but fortunately the compassionate nature of the heavenly Deliverer is to save. Those who trust Christ for salvation do not remain spiritually condemned. The Lord provides the beneficial work of the Holy Spirit within the believer's life through the sanctifying process of biblical conviction, which includes recurring repentance and inner peace through the Lord's gracious provision (**John 14:26-27**). For each day God gives us to live on this earth, we are allotted to choose for whom we will live. Will it be for the glory of God or the glory of self? When facing a crossroad, will you and I pick the unpopular narrow path that leads to life, strengthened by God's mercy (**Matthew 7:13-14**)? Be encouraged by the assuring words found in **Isaiah 50:9, "In truth, the Lord God will help me; who will condemn me?"**

In wrapping up our study of the nameless but known exonerated adulteress at the center, we are not privy to the choice she made following her merciful encounter with Jesus. Still, unanswered questions linger: Did she immediately obey Jesus' command and leave her life of sin? If married, did she seek to reconcile with her husband? Did her encounter with the Messiah persuade her to share her life-changing testimony with others residing in the same region? Was she among the group of grateful women who followed Jesus during His mission to take care of Him (**Mark 15:41**)? Perhaps the more pressing question is: *What daily choice(s) will you and I make because of the life-changing* *impact of God's mercy through Christ?* No one else in the crowd can make this decision for you or me, however, embracing God's mercy and sharing it with others is an excellent starting point.

## Application Acrostic

**C**ome to Jesus

**H**onor Christ as Lord

**O**pt for the way of escape from temptation

**I**nquire of the Lord for decisions

**C**onfess your sins

**E**mbrace God's mercy

## Thinking Through This

- When have you experienced a humiliating, shame-filled occurrence? How did you respond?
- What is the importance of confession of trespasses to the Lord and to others?
- Which of Jesus' three declarations (challenge, charity, charge) in response to the woman's sin resonates most with you and why?
- How can accepting Christ's mercy through salvation, versus remaining condemned in sin, make a difference in your life?

## Further Findings of God's Mercy

Read **John 5:1-16** to study the story of a *nameless but known* paralyzed man at the pool by the colonnade.

# Chapter 4

## THE MATERNAL WOMAN WITHIN THE REGION

*Forever His mercy stands, a boundless,*
*overwhelming immensity of divine pity and compassion.*

When my oldest son was in his last year of middle school, he joined the school's wrestling team. Though new to the sport, he had a successful season with "pins" and wins, since most of his opponents were younger and physically weaker than him. Once designated as the middle school's *Athlete of the Week* for his performance, my son's confidence grew alongside an increased desire to learn the necessary skills and competitive techniques for the one-on-one combat with his opponent in the circle on the wrestling mat. Throughout wrestling season, my husband and I spent many hours every Saturday anxiously anticipating our son's individual match. Each round lasted approximately three minutes or less, but to an anxious parent, those few minutes felt agonizing until the buzzer sounded and the round ended.

As my son reached his first year of high school, he decided to join the wrestling team again, but this time the competition level was very different. He recognized this change within the first couple weeks of practice. He was now considered the youngest, physically weakest, and least experienced among the competitors, which evoked an unfamiliar fear that chipped away at his initial confidence and gradually carried him to the brink of despair. He desired to quit the team, so as not to endure the inevitable pain and struggle, yet his original commitment to the coach and the team persuaded him to persevere and finish the grueling season, even if he lost every match.

I was frequently alarmed as a mother in the bleachers as I watched my adolescent son walk out alone onto a large wrestling mat to face his intimidating opponent. I freely admit that I did not like this arrangement at all. His combat attire consisted of only a thin singlet uniform, a pair of specialty grip wrestling shoes, and lightweight foam headgear, which offered limited protection. Neither his father nor I could assist our beloved child as he faced the fierce battle against his hefty contender, or recommend coaching tips from the stands. Most challenging, we could not prevent or protect our son from getting hurt during the challenging match. We could only watch from the sidelines, rely on the wrestling coach to care for our child, pray fervently on our son's behalf, and continue to cheer him on to fight hard to finish the struggle with the opposing foe. Moreover, we had to trust the wisdom of the only adult present within the wrestling ring alongside the competitors, the unidentified referee. I learned quickly that a victory is not always measured through a public win, but can be equally attributed to accomplishing a personal goal; for instance, concluding the round even when the outcome turns out differently than desired.

During my son's last few matches within that freshman year wrestling season, due to an unusual elimination process among the team, he was the last player left standing among his teammates. This meant that even though my son had not won enough matches to qualify for advancing to the major wrestling competitions, he was the unlikely contender to represent his high school in both the district and regional wrestling meets. My discouraged and weary firstborn was more than ready to be done with this temporary season of wrestling war, and so were his parents, but he technically was not the one who got to decide whether his season of struggle was over. That was wisely determined by his head coach, who had originally placed him in the tournament ring, and had a greater perspective on the purpose behind this public experience.

Each time my son entered the wrestling circle for his final matches during the championship events, since he was the lowest ranked competitor, unfortunately he had to face the highest ranked opponents. The mental battle proved to be a greater struggle than the physical fight because my child was keenly aware that he had no chance of winning before he ever stepped into the ring. He was outmatched every time by his rival, based on his inadequate skills, insufficient experience, weakened mental and physical stamina, and mounting personal fears. Nevertheless, with all the obstacles hindering him from victory, what made the difference was that my son stuck with it. He chose not to forfeit his matches but wrestled the best he could by utilizing prior preparation and trusting his coach to guide him as he navigated the enemy encounter.

Though beat up, worn out, and feeling despair, my son successfully completed that tough season still standing. He gained a fresh perspective on his season of struggle, even when the trial lasted longer than he wanted and turned out differently than he hoped. The Lord granted him and his parents mercy during that dreadful experience, attached to a cultivation of faith in God, whose presence remained with our family throughout the warfare. This resulted in internal peace while facing the conflict head-on, and with the unwavering support of others, no matter the outcome of the demanding competition.

It is one thing to reminisce about surviving a short-lived sporting event, but it is a frightening and daunting process to face an intense battle of spiritual warfare against a real and relentless enemy, like the destructive devil and his mighty army of disparaging demons. A desperate nameless but known MATERNAL WOMAN WITHIN THE

REGION understood this inherent battle her beloved daughter faced. She did not hesitate to fiercely fight for her child by approaching the only Savior who had unlimited power to save her little girl from a cruel adversary. Her biblical story is found in both **Mark 7:24-30** and **Matthew 15:21-28**, which is included below.

> ²¹ When Jesus left there, He withdrew to the area of Tyre and Sidon. ²² Just then a Canaanite woman from that region came and kept crying out, 'Have mercy on me, Lord, Son of David! My daughter is severely tormented by a demon.' ²³ Jesus did not say a word to her. His disciples approached Him and urged Him, 'Send her away because she's crying out after us.' ²⁴ He replied, 'I was sent only to the lost sheep of the house of Israel.' ²⁵ But she came, knelt before Him, and said, 'Lord, help me!' ²⁶ He answered, 'It isn't right to take the children's bread and throw it to the dogs.' ²⁷ 'Yes, Lord,' she said, 'yet even the dogs eat the crumbs that fall from their masters' table.' ²⁸ Then Jesus replied to her, 'Woman, your faith is great. Let it be done for you as you want.' And from that moment her daughter was healed.

When skimming through the details of this scriptural story, we learn that this mother was known by other characteristics, even though her name was not disclosed. She was a Canaanite (non-Jewish) and a Syrophoenician by birth, who resided in the region of Tyre and Sidon, a predominately Gentile territory north of Galilee. This was the area where Jesus chose to spend some much-needed time away from the crowd, yet He remained in the company of His original disciples. This purposeful pitstop followed days of active ministry near Galilee and Jerusalem, which included Jesus preaching God's Word, healing the sick, instructing His disciples, and opposing the religious leaders' complaints. **Mark 7** explains that Jesus entered a house to withdraw and did not want anyone to know where He was staying, but He could not escape notice.

Have you ever felt that way in your role as wife, mom, coworker, or ministry volunteer? You only want to be left alone—no additional needs to meet, questions to answer, people to face, or problems to solve. You just want to withdraw, relax, take a few breaths, and get refreshed, except there appears to be nowhere to go to escape those looking for you. What's a woman to do? Now, imagine if you were the incarnate perfect Son of the Living God who, among the public masses, had repeatedly shown His omnipotence, compassion, omniscience, and mightiness to save. There was always one more person who needed Jesus' help, sought out His power, wanted His time, yet He made the deliberate choice to take a brief break from it all.

There was no question that word got around about this unusual Rabbi wherever He went. People continued hearing the amazing stories about the marvelous works of God accomplished through this one man, Jesus. He was the divine-human Exceptional One who changed lives by a single touch, altered circumstances by speaking a word, taught the gospel message with authority, was drawn to the marginalized, did not cower to the demanding pressures from the religious folk, and whose holy presence caused the vilest demonic spirits to shriek with fear and beg Him for mercy.

If this Savior wandered into your small community, retreating at a neighbor's home, and you, the distressed parent of a tormented child suffering intensely under the domination of an evil spirit heard about Him, *what would you be willing to do to meet Jesus*? What barricades would you seek to knock down? With what obstacles would you contend to encounter this Redeemer? What hinderance would you move past to courageously approach Him and humbly plead for mercy? How many times would you beg Christ to intervene and deliver your debilitated child from their confined stronghold?

Put yourself in this unknown devoted mother's shoes, and then contemplate the resulting patient, lovingkindness of Jesus. He was receptive to her prayer and chose to fulfill her request for her ailing child, even though she technically imposed on His quiet time. Not only did Jesus do a mighty work in the life of this woman's daughter, but He used the opportunity to teach His disciples a valuable lesson about compassion in action through the observable faith of an unlikely candidate for mercy, thus superseding long-running racial barriers once again.

In studying this biblical story, the distraught, unnamed mother's encounter with Jesus illustrates four approaches to prayer for her troubled child. The first approach to prayer is: *a plea for mercy*.

The helpless mother's initial plea for mercy was for herself, for what she had endured in watching an evil presence oppress her daughter, with no way to stop it. The family needed someone greater and more powerful to redeem them, to halt the madness that was harmfully disrupting their household. Why this family, this mother, this little girl? Had this mom heard another parent's testimony of Christ's intervention for their demon-possessed child? We have no idea, but we do know this intentional woman did not hesitate to come to Jesus and express her specific petition concerning her daughter's serious problem. Her little girl, whom she doubtless loved more than life itself, was severely tormented by a demon. We don't know how long the child underwent this personal, possibly brutal torturous state, but make no mistake, this was an awful daily existence for the enslaved young girl and her concerned caretaker.

A demon, as referenced during the New Testament era, indicated an evil or unclean spirit, specifically an agent or companion of the devil who exercised evil power. The term, *demon-possessed*, characterized an afflicted person who was under the powerful control of a demon, typically displayed by abnormal behavior, and an intensely emotional alternate personality. Signs of demon-possession could show up in the form of physical deficits such as loss of speech, deafness, or blindness. The horrific physical condition could lead to constant restlessness and agitation, or involve the possessed person screaming repeatedly or crying out loudly. Other indicators may have included a form of unusual strength, unrestrained fierceness, or a violent convulsive seizure.

The Bible explains that during the brief earthly mission of Christ, demons believed Jesus was the Son of God and thus feared Him (**James 2:19**). Though they deliberately opposed Jesus' work, He still gloriously triumphed over their efforts. The devil and his demons were aware that they and Jesus belonged to two different spiritual kingdoms. Since these evil spirits knew *who* Jesus was, they were also aware of *what* He could do by His powerful word in casting them out with a single rebuke and driving them away, never to return (**Mark 1:34; Luke 4:41**). Furthermore, demons knew the truth about God, were familiar with God's commands, and often affirmed Jesus' deity and sinlessness when they were in the presence of Jesus. Regardless, they chose to deny the truth and reject the Lord God. Therefore, demons and the devil are spiritual beings eternally condemned to the hellish abyss of judgment (**Revelation 18:2, 8**). We can only speculate how demon-possession happens to an individual, but we know the only cure for deliverance from the wicked dominion of darkness is God's mercy in the powerful name of Jesus Christ.

Let's remain alert and be aware that the deceptive devil and his team of persuasive evil spirits still exist today and enact harmful deeds among humanity with a central agenda to steal, kill, and destroy God's creation (**John 8:44; 1 Timothy 4:1-2**). Remember, though, that the sovereign Yahweh reigns and rules supremely with all authority over all things, including created beings, such as demons and the devil (**Matthew 28:18**). We won't fully comprehend on this side of eternity how God's sovereignty and evil spirits coexist within a broken world; we must understand that only Jesus can rescue and redeem people from the enemy. Let us continue to trust the Lord and look to the Scriptures to better understand the unfathomable power of God that prevails amid evil forces (**John 10:10**). Don't stop praying and pleading for God's mercy for you and your loved ones who may be living under the tempting sway of the evil one (**1 John 5:19**). The defeated adversary of God knows his time on earth is short, which makes his furious mayhem widely worse (**Revelation 12:12**).

In this biblical mother-daughter scenario, the narrative began with a plea for mercy to God from a distressed parent tending to her suffering child. By launching your prayer approach with an appeal for God's mercy, you humbly admit that you cannot fix the prevailing issue(s) penetrating your son or daughter's life, but you can certainly petition their Creator, as articulated in **Psalm 116:1, "I love the Lord because He has heard my appeal for mercy."**

Upon making a plea for mercy, the second approach to prayer modeled by the unidentified woman is: *a persistent request*. The determined mother's request to Jesus was a recurrent and deliberate cry of desperation for Him to rescue her daughter from a horrible affliction. This fervent momma was so insistent to gain the attention of Jesus, that she irritated Jesus' close disciples witnessing this scene. They viewed this female foreigner as a bother to their much-needed respite, but her insistence in voicing her child's crisis burdened the tender heart of God's Son. The mother desired Jesus—the only known Source for an effective remedy—to cast out the demon from her daughter, but the annoyed disciples wanted her to go away and deal with her plight by herself. Mysteriously, Jesus' initial response to both the wailing mother and His irritated disciples was to remain silent.

The disciples' inconsiderate reaction to the woman did not deter her from seeking the Jewish Messiah, who was sent through the Davidic line of the chosen Hebrew nation. As indicated by Jesus within the biblical text of Matthew 15, the Son of Man was sent first to feed the lost sheep of Israel, with spiritual living water and the bread of life by grace through faith. But He was likewise sent to extend the same gospel invitation to lost Gentiles, also by grace through faith in the name of Jesus (**John 1:10-12**). There was mounting animosity among multiple generations of combined Israelites and Gentiles, a dividing wall of hostility that Christ would soon obliterate by His death and subsequent resurrection (**Ephesians 2:13-14**).

Biblical Gentiles were often referred to by the derogatory slur, "dogs", by the Jewish descendants, indicating a lowly family pet waiting under the table for scraps of food to fall to the ground. Nevertheless, the "dog" label was ignorantly and incorrectly viewed by some as divine proof of God's disfavor, which prompted contempt by Jewish-raised religious people towards so-called Gentile outsiders. Jesus subtly referenced this label in the presence of His disciples to shed light on their hidden prejudice toward the female stranger, which sadly dissuaded them from offering an empathetic response. Thankfully, Jesus showed that compassion breaks down obstacles and shatters divisions by getting to the heart of the matter, which is the essential care for another human being made in the image of God, regardless of their ethnicity. **Philippians 2:3** exhorts the New Testament believers, **"…in humility consider others as more important than yourselves."**

The disciples' naïve and narrow view of Jesus' divine ministry and redemptive mission caused them to think that His purpose was limited to one ethnic group, rather than expanded to impact the diverse human race for those who would believe His message. On this occasion, the anonymous mother did not allow a presumed offensive name to prevent her from pursuing the Messiah, nor view it as merit for a defensive rebuttal. Rather, she prioritized calling out to the One and Only Name that mattered, Jesus Christ. **Psalm 9:10** declares, **"Those who know Your name trust in You because You have not abandoned those who seek You, Lord."** Ironically, it was not His close followers, but the unfamiliar Gentile who quickly acknowledged the Messiah as Lord, Son of David, and Master within this moment. She believed only Jesus could provide the life-changing response necessary to heal her daughter from her infirmity, even if He decided otherwise.

May you and I continue to fervently and patiently petition the Mighty God to intervene and save the lives of our beloved friends and relatives. Believe Yahweh can do it, without acting as if He owes you anything whatsoever to fulfill your request. The Lord is God. He hears your cry of affliction, He sees your heartache, He observes your misery, He knows your suffering, and He sent His Son Jesus to rescue and redeem individuals from the power of the enemy. His divine presence remains through the indwelling Holy Spirit for those who believe in Him for salvation (**Exodus 3:7-10**).

**Psalm 72:12-14** describes the wonders of the Lord God, **"For He will rescue the poor who cry out and the afflicted who have no helper. He will have pity on the poor and helpless and save the lives of the poor. He will redeem them from oppression and violence, for their lives are precious in His sight."** The Lord cares for the spiritual well-being of your precious child, even more than you do as their committed parent. Put on "the full armor of God", relying on His strength, as you battle the brutal spiritual warfare together with your child to stand up against the crafty schemes of the devil. Do not hesitate to take up the reliable "shield of faith" and utilize the "sharp sword of the Spirit", God's Word, as you pray in the Spirit with every prayer request (**Ephesians 6:10-18**).

When we come before the Lord in prayer, it should naturally include praise and thanksgiving for *Who* God is, along with our confession of sin. Because of *what* He is able to do on your behalf, prayer also is meant to be direct communication with the heavenly Father in voicing specific requests. **Philippians 4:6-7** exhorts, **"Don't worry about anything, but in everything, through prayer and**

**petition with thanksgiving, present your requests to God. And the peace of God, which surpasses all understanding, will guard your hearts and minds in Christ Jesus."** This petitioning approach is not meant to be a misguided, manipulative *name it-claim it* philosophy of prayer as presuming upon God or seeking to obligate Him to give you what you ask for. Rather, you are humbly seeking the will of God, while being precise in your plea, exhibiting a trust in the timing and provision of your request based on God's wisdom and purpose. Your eager waiting with patience and hope for the Lord's will to unfold regarding your precise request can provide peace that surpasses understanding.

Remain confident in God's ability to fulfill the request, whether He does or not, and acknowledge your need for God to handle this predicament since you have run out of options. Thankfully, we also have the Holy Spirit to help us in our weaknesses, when we don't know what to pray for or how. He intercedes in prayer in accordance with the will of God (**Romans 8:26-27**).

Once the unknown mother approached Jesus with a plea for mercy before she gave her persistent request, we observe her third approach to prayer as: *a posture of surrender*. She knelt at the feet of Jesus and asserted three powerful words of submission, **"Lord, help me!"** This type of posture and simple prayer may be the only way you can exercise feeble faith with limited strength to verbalize to God your desperate need for help. Even if you don't receive the immediate solution you asked for your problem, something greater occurs, which is your drawing near to God's presence as He mercifully draws closer to you. **James 4:7-8** exhorts, **"Submit to God. Resist the devil, and he will flee from you. Draw near to God, and He will draw near to you."**

Surrendering to Christ's lordship indicates that you desire to release personal control over your wishes for your son or daughter and fully trust God for His unfolding plan for His glory in your child's life. The posture of the despairing parent was surrendering and falling at the feet of Jesus as she pled for her daughter's relief from the torturous grasp of the unclean spirit. Desperation can drive a person to their knees, earnestly petitioning the heavenly Father, even if the person has only heard about God, but has not been directly impacted by His Word, until that moment. A parent's anguish over their child's health can build the parent's faith in the power of God. The Lord knows a person's heart, understands their desires, and is concerned about their needs. This, however, was not only a matter of a daughter's physical and spiritual redemption, but also a mother's increased awareness of her continuous need to rely on God and His Word in all family matters.

Jesus also modeled a posture of surrender one momentous night when kneeling alone in a garden before His heavenly Father and voicing a precise request out of the anguish He experienced. This was prior to His arrest, which was followed by His crucifixion to absorb the wrath of God on behalf of sinners' transgressions. Captured in **Luke 22:42**, the blameless Son of God prayed, **"Father, if You are willing, take this cup away from Me – nevertheless, not My will, but Yours, be done."** This complemented Jesus' previous teaching to His disciples when they asked Him, **"Lord, teach us to pray" (Luke 11:1)**. Jesus taught them that whenever His followers prayed, they should pray like this, **"Our Father in heaven, Your name be honored as holy. Your kingdom come. Your will be done on earth as it is in heaven. Give us today our daily bread. And forgive us our debts, as we also have forgiven our debtors. And do not bring us into temptation, but deliver us from the evil one" (Matthew 6:9-13)**.

No matter the age or stage of your child, may you continue to pray on their behalf for God's Name to be honored, for His will to be done, for His daily provision to be given, for forgiveness of your child's debts, and that the Lord would lead them away from temptation to deliver them completely from the evil one's destruction.

The mother's approach to petitioning Jesus began with a plea for mercy and followed by a persistent request, then shifted into a posture of surrender before her fourth approach to prayer concluded with: <u>a profession of faith</u>.

A profession of your faith in the sovereignty of the Creator and Sustainer of the world, the Maker of your child, demonstrates your firm conviction that anything is possible for those who believe in Christ. Conversely, it also includes accepting that it is possible that God's answer to your request in response to your faith may look different than you had originally hoped or planned. Still, may your faith remain steady in the Lord and His Word, and in His purpose-filled plans for the duration of your child's earthly life. **James 5:15** declares, **"The prayer of faith will save the sick person, and the Lord will raise him up; if he has committed sins, he will be forgiven."** This verse addresses spiritual sickness more than physical sickness, but even so, we are reminded to pray with genuine faith on behalf of others who may be too sick to pray or too doubtful to exercise faith. Pour out your urgent complaint before God and reveal your severe trouble to Him. God's merciful answer to your prayer request may be, "Yes, No, or Wait, not now," but continue to trust Him, believe His Word, and rest in His presence as you surrender your desires and entrust your child's life into God's capable hands.

Once Jesus affirmed the mother's "great faith," she took Him at His word, as demonstrated in her willingness to receive a morsel of bread from His table, trusting His pronounced promise, and returning home to where her suffering daughter lay. This grateful mom found that her daughter had been completely released from the enemy's grip and restored; the child was obviously well. The demonic influence had been immediately removed and no longer had divine permission to reside in their family's household. Praise God!

**Luke 11:9-10** records a teaching session by Jesus, who asked a fascinating rhetorical question to well-meaning parents when addressing the subject of persistent prayer by faith in the Lord. Jesus emphasized the value of frequently petitioning the heavenly Father for the concerns weighing heavily on a person's heart. **"Ask, and it will be given to you. Seek, and you will find. Knock, and the door will be opened to you."** Then Jesus reminded those listening to His message about the most important request a caring, but imperfect parent could make for their son or daughter before the Lord: **"If you then, who are evil, know how to give good gifts to your children, how much more will the heavenly Father give the Holy Spirit to those who ask Him?"** (v. 13). A child's primary and ultimate need is the same as a parent's primary and ultimate need: Salvation through Jesus Christ by the power of the indwelling Holy Spirit.

God's matchless mercy changes lives by cleansing and purging the sinfulness that has defiled parents and consumed their depraved children. Jesus' lovingkindness through His Word can pervade your household, generate peace within your family, and righteously impact the lives of the next generation. Continue to approach the throne of grace with confidence and pray for your children's physical, emotional, psychological, relational, and most importantly, spiritual well-being. To God be the glory forever!

In closing this chapter and considering the ramifications of this nameless but known mother's astonishing encounter with Jesus, perhaps your son or daughter may be battling powerful demons of their own. Possibly the ferocious fiend that is devouring your teenager is in the form of recurring addiction or has spurred other damaging behaviors, thus harmfully influencing their current decisions. Perhaps your son or daughter has been heavily swayed to engage in worldly temptations and pervasive, corrupt culture that have enticed their fleshly desires. They may be under the heavy persuasion of false teaching and deceptive lies by those who have rejected the things of God. Maybe your child is plagued by encroaching disappointment over personal performance, or overwhelmed with anxiety, or distraught with depression, all of which make interpersonal relationships challenging, not to mention day-to-day living and faith in Jesus Christ.

In the current age of prevalent social media—which can be a beneficial instrument for good, or a toxic agent of destruction for our younger generation—the spiritual battles for the hearts and minds of our sons or daughters is extremely intense. We cannot fight this battle alone on behalf of our children; we need Jesus, His power, His truth, the support of others, and endurance to persistently pray for and encourage our vulnerable, confused children. This fierce fight for them begins on our knees, surrendering before God by faith, asking Him to intervene on behalf of our cherished children by opening their hearts and minds and drawing them to Jesus through the life-changing gospel message from His Word.

There is something heart-wrenching that defies logic and reaches beyond racial, socioeconomic, or religious boundaries when witnessing a distraught parent desperately pleading for their tormented child to be delivered by a perceived savior. A well-meaning parent has been known to offer everything they have, including their own life, to spare their child from any further dreadful suffering. Do we have the same resolve to tenaciously seek the mercy of Jesus, asking for wisdom for how best to help our children in their spiritual battle? We cannot spiritually save our sons and daughters; only Christ can do that. We can come alongside them, point them to the Savior, and earnestly pray that they know, believe, and wholly follow Jesus and His Word throughout their lifetimes.

May we never underestimate the remarkable impact of God's matchless mercy through Jesus within our households, which can produce thankful memories among our family members, and regularly remind us of the vast goodness and faithfulness of the Lord. **"Blessed be the Lord, for He has heard the sound of my pleading. The Lord is my strength and my shield; my heart trusts in Him, and**

I am helped. Therefore my heart celebrates, and I give thanks to Him with my song" (Psalm 28:6-7).

**Application Acrostic**

**F**all at the feet of Jesus in surrender

**A**sk your specific request(s) without hesitation

**I**mmerse yourself in God's Word

**T**rust God for His answers

**H**alt from worrying and pray instead

**Thinking Through This**

- How do you typically approach the Lord when petitioning Him?
- How do you generally respond when your petition to God is not immediately answered? How have you previously reacted when God's will unfolded differently than your original plea?
- If you are a parent, what is the most recent prayer request you have made to God on behalf of your child and why?
- When do you find it most difficult to trust God with concerns for your child's well-being?

**Further Findings of God's Mercy**

Read **Mark 9:14-29** and **Luke 9:37-43** to study the story of a *nameless but known* father and his demon-possessed son among a crowd near the mountain.

# Chapter 5

## THE SINFUL WOMAN AROUND THE TOWN

*Nothing can increase, diminish, or alter the quality of God's mercy.*

In her best-selling book, *The Hiding Place*©, author Corrie ten Boom concludes the final chapter with the story of a memorable encounter she had with an unlikely individual, a former German guard during World War II, from whom she had endured cruel abuse during her captivity in a Nazi concentration camp. The Lord used this unforeseen meeting to expand her perspective on the extent of Jesus' love and forgiveness toward the undeserving. Corrie and her family secretly worked against the inhumane Nazi agenda by hiding Jews in their home in Holland, until the German militia there uncovered their hideout strategy. As punishment, the ten Boom family was transported to Ravensbrück concentration camp, an unimaginably dreadful place where Corrie's sister (Betsie) and their father died after suffering at the hands of their harsh captors.

Fast forward years later to find a liberated Corrie delivering a gospel-centered message of hope and forgiveness to a church body in Munich, Germany. There, she recognized a former German SS man attending the worship service. He was the jailer who had stood guard at the female inmates' shower room door in the processing center at Ravensbrück. Corrie further described this surprising scene:

> He was the first of our actual jailers that I had seen since that time. And suddenly it was all there – the roomful of mocking men, the heaps of clothing, Betsie's pain-blanched face.
>
> He came up to me as the church was emptying, beaming and bowing. 'How grateful I am for your message, *Fraulein*.' He said, 'To think that, as you say, He has washed my sins away!'
>
> His hand was thrust out to shake mine. And I, who preached so often to the people in Bloemendaal the need to forgive, kept my hand at my side.
>
> Even as the angry, vengeful thoughts boiled through me, I saw the sin of them. Jesus Christ had died for this man; was I going to ask for more? Lord Jesus, I prayed, forgive me and help me to forgive him.
>
> I tried to smile; I struggled to raise my hand. I could not. I felt nothing, not the slightest spark of warmth or charity. And so again I breathed a silent prayer. Jesus, I cannot forgive him. Give me Your forgiveness.
>
> As I took his hand the most incredible thing happened. From my shoulder along my arm and through my hand a current seemed to pass from me to him, while into my heart sprang a love for this stranger that almost overwhelmed me.
>
> And so I discovered that it is not on our forgiveness any more than on our goodness that the world's healing hinges, but on

His. When He tells us to love our enemies, along with the command, He gives us the love itself. It took a lot of love.[7]

Loving sacrificially as a Christ-follower is not a simple act to practice; it is not based on how we feel, but rather about honoring Jesus by demonstrating our unconditional commitment to another's well-being. Corrie ten Boom's true story illustrates this principle effectively, and provides awareness of the direct correlation between sacrificial love and genuine forgiveness. **First John 1:9**, reminds believers to love others because we have first been loved by our Savior. Moreover, **Ephesians 4:32** exhorts Christ-followers, **"Be kind and compassionate to one another, forgiving one another, just as God also forgave you in Christ."**

Love and forgiveness complement one another. It's difficult to sincerely love someone who has hurt you and not also offer them forgiveness at the same time. Similarly, it is tough to truly forgive someone apart from a change of heart through the work of Christ, who loves and has forgiven both you and me, although we have sinned against Him.

**Proverbs 10:12** says, **"Hatred stirs up conflict, but love covers all offenses."** Furthermore, **1 Peter 4:8** exhorts, **"Above all, maintain constant love for one another since love covers a multitude of sins."** These verses are not suggesting that we bypass wisdom and discernment when responding to the offender and their offense against us. Nor are they indicating that we dismiss, ignore, or remain in a setting of abuse. A response of love or forgiveness is a choice with equal value; together they demonstrate God's mercy, which can powerfully change a person or alter a situation for the better. As fallen but redeemed people, believers still battle with their sinful default mode to hate and hold a grudge toward another when wounded by them. Responding with love and forgiveness instead is counterintuitive,

---

[7] Corrie ten Boom and John and Elizabeth Sherrill, *The Hiding Place* (Old Tappan, NJ: Spire Books, 1971), 238.

a supernatural work of the Holy Spirit, which is why many are surprised by this type of response. Others don't understand the reason behind an alternate reaction to retaliation when revenge seems warranted.

The *Holman Concise Bible Dictionary*© defines forgiveness as: "The gracious act of God by which believers are put into a right relationship to God and transferred from spiritual death to spiritual life through the sacrifice of Jesus. It is also the ongoing gift of God without which our lives as Christians would be 'out of joint' and full of guilt. In terms of a human dimension, forgiveness is that first restorative act and attitude toward those who have wronged us that restores relationships and fellowship."[8]

One cannot appreciate the practice of forgiveness without also understanding real repentance, which is an essential biblical concept. Repentance was discussed in a previous chapter, but I believe it's helpful to reiterate characteristics of repentance in light of the unnamed woman referenced in this chapter. Repentance is defined as: "A feeling of regret, a changing of the mind, or a turning from sin to God...a reorientation of the sinner to God...making a radical change within the heart, turning from sin and at the same time turning to God. Such a turning, or conversion was openly manifested in justice, kindness, and humility."[9] The gospel message of salvation continues to urge the sinner to repent of their sin, believe in God's Word, and love and follow Jesus wholeheartedly.

The Bible further explains the vital process of repentance: First, God's kindness toward us is intended to lead us to repentance (**Roman 2:4**). Then, repentance leads us to the knowledge of the truth of God (**2 Timothy 2:25**). Finally, repentance leads us to salvation without regret by grace through faith in Christ (**2 Corinthians 7:10**). Remarkably, even one sinner's repentance produces exuberant joy in

---

[8] Trent C. Butler, editor, *Holman Concise Bible Dictionary* (Nashville, TN: Broadman & Holman Publishers, 2001), 242.

[9] Trent C. Butler, Ibid, 527.

heaven among the angels (**Luke 15:7**). May we never underestimate the importance of repentance, since it often precedes forgiveness spurred by a heart of love.

In the biblical account of the nameless but known SINFUL WOMAN AROUND THE TOWN, her story slightly differs from those of the other unnamed women. This woman initiated her encounter with Jesus to tangibly express her devotion to Christ because of His love and forgiveness first shown to her. Moreover, Jesus used the occasion to teach a vital lesson to a prominent leader within the man's home during a dinner party the man hosted for the honored guest. When the unwelcome intruder arrived at the event, her presence altered the course of the evening. The narrative is found in **Luke 7:36-50**:

> **36 Then one of the Pharisees invited Him to eat with him. He entered the Pharisee's house and reclined at the table. 37 And a woman in the town who was a sinner found out that Jesus was reclining at the table in the Pharisee's house. She brought an alabaster jar of perfume 38 and stood behind Him at His feet, weeping, and began to wash His feet with her tears. She wiped His feet with her hair, kissing them and anointing them with the perfume. 39 When the Pharisee who had invited Him saw this, he said to himself, 'This man, if He were a Prophet, would know who and what kind of woman this is who is touching Him—she's a sinner!' 40 Jesus replied to him, 'Simon, I have something to say to you.' He said, 'Say it, Teacher.'**
>
> **41 'A creditor had two debtors. One owed five hundred denarii, and the other fifty. 42 Since they could not pay it back, he graciously forgave them both. So, which of them**

will love him more?' ⁴³ Simon answered, 'I suppose the one he forgave more.' 'You have judged correctly,' He told him.⁴⁴ Turning to the woman, He said to Simon, 'Do you see this woman? I entered your house; you gave Me no water for My feet, but she, with her tears, has washed My feet and wiped them with her hair. ⁴⁵ You gave Me no kiss, but she hasn't stopped kissing My feet since I came in. ⁴⁶ You didn't anoint My head with olive oil, but she has anointed My feet with perfume. ⁴⁷ Therefore I tell you, her many sins have been forgiven; that's why she loved much. But the one who is forgiven little, loves little.' ⁴⁸ Then He said to her, 'Your sins are forgiven.' ⁴⁹ Those who were at the table with Him began to say among themselves, 'Who is this man who even forgives sins?' ⁵⁰ And He said to the woman, 'Your faith has saved you. Go in peace.'**

This Luke 7 passage has the topic subheading, "much forgiveness, much love" in some Bibles. Perhaps this signifies a correlation between these two responses to cultivate a harmonious relationship. Some people require receiving more acts of forgiveness for themselves, strictly based on the number of trespasses they have committed. In turn, this can fuel the strength of their love toward the compassionate forgiver even more. As we study this biblical story, we will observe how it characterizes the matchless mercy of God.

We learn of the forgiveness of a determined, faith-filled, female sinner, whose name is not revealed, but whose habitual sinful actions were exposed, resulting in a defiled reputation around town. She could be the poster child for "the lost one" whom Christ came to seek and save, and be eternally changed by God's mercy. Jesus' ministry fortunately included receiving and saving sinners; yet He earned the reputation from His persecutors of being a friend of sinners (**Matthew 2:15-16; Luke 7:34**). In the context of this sinful woman's story, the term "sinner" was often lumped in with a despised tax collector and implied a criminal class of people who were typically known for making a living by engaging in lewdness or lawless deeds.

Thankfully this unidentified, but renewed woman's biblical narrative teaches five principles about sacrificial love and frequent forgiveness, effectively practiced within interpersonal relationships. The first principle illustrated is: <u>*loving and forgiving can extend beyond close relatives or friends to reach strangers*</u>. This is revealed at the start of the story when Jesus received a cordial invitation from an obviously unwelcoming host.

Throughout different villages within Israel, Jesus spent time traveling and proclaiming the Good News of the Kingdom of God to the crowds. His earthly ministry impacted many diverse peoples and groups, which included fishermen, government officials, religious leaders, women of different ages and stages, tax collectors, the rich, the poor, the disabled, the desperate, and the notorious, defiled sinners. He was known for being a powerful Prophet and an amazing Teacher, based on His preaching style, healing ministry, and the public and less obvious miracles He performed. Jesus' scriptural intelligence was acknowledged by the religious leaders, like the Pharisees, who were considered the most important and numerous of religious groups, and exercised control over the local synagogues. In addition, this sect often separated themselves from the masses to study and interpret the Old Testament Law with little interest in government politics. Prior to this dinner party, Jesus preached a sermon, recorded in **Luke 6:27-36**, by which He addressed the matter of loving your enemies and showing them mercy, even when they have treated you poorly. He remarked that this was a tougher task in contrast to loving those who love in return and have done good to you.

As mentioned in Luke 7, one particular Pharisee invited the renown Messiah to dine with him and Jesus graciously accepted the invitation. We quickly learn that the host failed to provide even the basic elements of customary Jewish hospitality to welcome Jesus upon first entering his home. **Hebrews 13:1-2** encourages, **"Let brotherly love continue. Don't neglect to show hospitality, for by doing this some have welcomed angels as guests without knowing it."** Sadly, the aloof host overlooked the privilege afforded to him to have God's Son reclining at his table.

Perhaps this skeptical leader, named Simon, was distracted and forgot about cordial traditions in his zeal to ask questions of this Prophet. Perhaps he or his family and household were caught up in the reflected glory of this Prophet merely entering their home. Jesus had drawn much attention from the neighboring townsfolk, so this Pharisee was curious, as were so many. Jesus eventually pointed out Simon's lack of common courtesy, but He waited until an uninvited person arrived to the event, a person Simon regarded as repulsive. Still, she demonstrated the simple, contrasting example of humility by her worshipful posture in the presence of Jesus, thus trampling the culture's acceptable social manners. This unnamed female's story begins by emphasizing that love and forgiveness can extend beyond family and friends to reach distant strangers.

The second central principle found in this sinful woman's saga is: <u>*loving and forgiving includes an outpouring of tangible actions to serve others*</u>. This was demonstrated when the unwelcomed woman dramatically anointed the feet of Jesus.

As dinner was underway for Jesus and Simon, along with other invited guests, the unexpected visitor made her way into the site of this social gathering. Jesus rarely extended His stay in one place before moving on to the next town, so this reviled stranger perhaps believed this might be her only chance to meet the merciful Teacher.

She brought with her the knowledge that her life had apparently been changed through Jesus' gracious offer of eternal life to *whomever* would believe in Him (**John 3:16-17**). Presumably, she was the kind of woman who "got around" the town; most likely a prostitute, thus labeled by her immoral reputation, so this was an offensive intrusion for the lackadaisical host, Simon. I suspect her goal was not to make a spectacle of herself at the dinner party, but to make much of Jesus. Notably, the woman never spoke a word during this unusual encounter, but her actions spoke louder than words; her humility and gratitude spoke volumes. Yes, this woman's unsolicited presence at the table changed the tone of this unforgettable scene, and her remarkable story continues to be told throughout multiple generations.

We don't know much about this lady's background but we can speculate what her life was like *before* meeting Jesus and deduce how her life was different *after* she met Jesus. We can further decipher the purpose for this woman seeking out Christ: to offer Him a precious gift symbolic of her devoted love to her Savior. Just as she had very likely elbowed and pushed her way to the table of honor, this daring woman defied social norms, and also pushed through her fears of what others thought of her. She laid aside her guilt and shame and sought her merciful Messiah. Who else but God's Son had the power and compassion to forgive and redeem a sinful woman like her?

As we glimpse into what quickly became an extremely uncomfortable household setting, note that Jesus was not rattled by this woman's sudden display of appropriate affection, even if onlookers felt embarrassed. The party was just getting started when this awkward scenario unfolded, and then proceeded until the sinful, but pardoned woman left that party in peace, leaving the disgruntled host and other attendees to contemplate Jesus' teaching about love and forgiveness.

A cold-shouldered public setting did not deter the nameless woman from kneeling down in surrender to Christ; He, of course, already knew her. This was her tangible expression of tender worship to the only One worthy of all her praise. Breaking a costly alabaster flask that contained expensive ointment, then pouring it out on the feet of Christ with tears gushing from her eyes and snot dripping from her nose, was worth the cost she'd borne to honor Him. She had no towel with her for drying His feet, but perhaps her hair represented a softer, better, more personal object for this intimate moment. Would any other woman have done something similar, for even one person, at any time, in any place, for any other reason? Jesus accepted this woman for who she was, a sinner in need of God's grace, and He was sufficiently able to rescue her from a past immoral life and grant her a new purified life. This former sinful woman around the town, now a thankful servant of Jesus within the house, had a renewed testimony of spiritual transformation to tell others because of the mercy offered by the kind Master.

Toward the end of His earthly ministry, just prior to His crucifixion, Jesus exhibited a similar example of servanthood in the presence of His closest disciples reclining at a table, sharing the Last Supper, in an Upper Room. John 13 explains that Jesus rose from the table, laid aside His outer garment, took a towel and tied it around His waist, poured water in a basin, and then proceeded to wash and dry each disciple's feet. The sequence of this foot washing during the dinner may have included His washing the feet of Judas Iscariot, Christ's publicly known betrayer (**John 6:70-71**). After Jesus finished engaging in this menial task always designated for the lowliest of servants within a host's home, Jesus resumed His place at the table alongside His chosen disciples. He then asked them a question followed by a directive: **"Do you know what I have done for you? You call Me Teacher and Lord – and you are speaking rightly, since that is what I am. So if I, your Lord and Teacher have washed your feet, you also ought to wash one another's feet. For I have given you an example, that you also should do just as I have done for you" (John 13:12-15)**. Are we also following Jesus' tender-hearted example in serving others through an outpouring of tangible actions? The worshipful woman modeled well her Savior's pattern.

This moves us forward to the third principle tied to loving sacrificially and forgiving repeatedly: *loving and forgiving may require confrontation or involve uncomfortable moments*. This is observed when Jesus confronted the private thoughts of Simon the host. The Pharisee witnessed this shocking scene of the nameless but known lady emotionally, dramatically, and openly anointing the feet of Jesus, yet Simon did not speak. The Bible records his private thoughts which included his critical perspective of Jesus and his disparaging outlook on the woman. Though this expert in the Law did not inquire out loud about Jesus' role as Prophet, he quietly questioned the Messiah's prophetic capability to know what kind of woman He had permitted to touch Him. Instantly, Jesus gently confronted those private thoughts by using his personal name to address him, **"Simon, I have something to say to you" (Luke 7:40)**. Did Simon only hear the Messiah's voice or opt to listen and learn from His words? Simon's name lived on; the woman's did not.

Jesus chose to use a parable to instruct Simon, pointing out the example of the unidentified guest. Christ's telling of the fable confirmed that He was mindful of Simon's hidden thoughts and concealed sins, perhaps considered *minor* to most; yet Jesus was equally aware of this woman's prior disgraceful sins, possibly classified as *major* by many. Either way, Jesus clearly pointed out that no matter the amount owed by a bankrupt debtor (a slave to the lender), repayment was costly; neither had the means to reimburse the righteous creditor. **James 2:8-10** explains, **"Indeed, if you fulfill the royal law prescribed in the Scripture, 'Love your neighbor as yourself,' you are doing well. If, however, you show favoritism, you commit sin and are convicted by the law as transgressors. For whoever keeps the entire law and yet stumbles at one point, is guilty of breaking it all."** Shortly after sharing the parable in Luke 7, Jesus further astounded those listening to His lesson by declaring His authority to forgive the sins of the woman.

Whether we break one commandment from God or transgress multiple laws, according to the parable, the only way we can cover the debt is through a declaration by the merciful debt-collector to cancel the debt with the unearned gift of forgiveness. Only then would either debtor be free from the burden of the penalty required, and in turn, be granted a choice of how they respond to the giver of the costly gift. Would this surprising turn of events motivate either nonpayer, represented in the parable, to love the one who cancelled their debt even more? Could either debtor grasp what their creditor's kindness spared them? Simon rightly answered Jesus' question, yet misjudged the woman. At the same time, he underestimated the extent of God's mercy to forgive trespasses; he did not think to appraise the depth of his own sinful condition.

When pride and self-righteousness are present within our hearts, thoughts, and attitudes, we neglect to bow before the divine Master in humbled submission because we ignore our desperate need for the Savior. God has provided a way through His beloved Son to have direct access to Him, even though sin has separated us and fractured that relationship. We must first admit our need for a Savior to rescue us. Only Jesus has the power to save a sinner, whether a prominent Pharisee or an unnamed but unforgettable prostitute. **Romans 5:6-8** reminds us, **"For while we were still helpless, at the right time, Christ died for the ungodly. For rarely will someone die for a just person – though for a good person perhaps someone might even dare to die. But God proves His own love for us in that while we were still sinners, Christ died for us."**

Jesus continued His confrontative, perhaps uncomfortable dialogue with Simon in front of the curious attendees, which further involved the noble example of the least likely person in the room. This brings us to the fourth principle of sacrificial love and recurring forgiveness: <u>*loving and forgiving another person does not dismiss their sin, but acknowledges their desperate need for a Savior*</u>. We notice this when Jesus openly and clearly commended the public conduct of the female visitor while she demonstrated her adoration for the Messiah.

Throughout the Gospels, Jesus often asked a question in a group setting that naturally resulted in an obvious answer. To those who were listening to His teaching during this event, the verbal exchange between Simon and Him was no exception. While Jesus turned toward the kneeling woman to acknowledge her presence and emphasize her display of worship, He spoke directly to Simon in **Luke 7:44** and inquired, **"Do you see this woman?"** It's a comical question; who in the room did NOT see her? However, Jesus was preparing to make a point of contrast in commending the woman's public honorable behavior, while at the same time confronting the host's private disapproval. Since Simon acted more bothered by the woman's existence in his earthly home rather than burdened for her future eternity in a heavenly home, his skewed perspective affected his attitude toward the Savior.

Jesus addressed two opposite responses demonstrated within one setting, which included the host's neglect of common courtesy to the honored guest, versus the uninvited woman's outpouring of devotion to her revered Lord. The contrast is quite appalling – a disparaged individual from the red-light district choosing to honor and worship the Lord of Lords, as opposed to an esteemed leader failing to show minimal kindness to the King of Kings. If we get sidetracked by focusing on a person's past mistakes, then we may miss celebrating their future opportunities because of the redeeming work of Christ in their life. **Ephesians 1:7-8** declares the sacrificial love of the Father through Jesus the Son, **"In Him we have redemption through His blood, the forgiveness of our trespasses, according to the riches of His grace that He richly poured out on us with all wisdom and understanding."**

The woman was changed by the matchless mercy of God and desired to be near her divine Redeemer. She wanted to clearly show Him her love, commitment, and gratitude for His grace and mercy that cleansed her from all unrighteousness. It is evident that she believed in Jesus and surrendered her life to Him, which impacted her moment of worship during the party and subsequently changed the course of her life. To be clear, the nameless but known woman's public act did not save her, as salvation comes by God's grace through faith in Christ alone. However, her external demonstration declared the internal change of heart as proof of her faith and following of Jesus. He commended her for that, rather than condemning her trespasses. Christ did not dismiss her many sins, but she recognized her need for a Savior; she sought Him out, received His forgiveness, placed her faith in Him, and honored her Redeemer.

It is tough to forgive, especially repeatedly; it does not come naturally. We often question how many times we should forgive the same offense or the same offender, since we don't want to enable a person to continue to hurt us, nor be subjected to feeling that they are somehow "getting away with" sinning against us. However, we also understand that unforgiveness can be just as detrimental. Forgiveness takes time and requires patience, practice, and prayer, but a genuine Christ-follower, like Christ, continues to love others and not cease to forgive them. In doing so, not only do we model our Savior, but also we glorify our Father.

Finally, we conclude with the fifth mercy-filled principle of loving sacrificially and forgiving repeatedly: <u>*loving and forgiving others is possible when we embrace the depth of God's love and forgiveness granted to us*</u>.

Jesus provided an abrupt finale to this dinner event by verbally clarifying the unwelcome woman's motivation for her love-filled actions, versus the insincere host's lack-of-love displayed by his inaction. The Messiah reinforced to both the woman and Simon that *her* many sins were indeed forgiven for good. Jesus did not deny the woman possibly had a rap sheet of immoral offenses, but instead, the gathered group needed to comprehend the lengths to which God's forgiveness extends to cover all the sins of a repentant sinner, past – present – future. This in turn should spur the one who has been forgiven by this merciful gift to passionately love and obey God.

By the power of the indwelling Holy Spirit, a redeemed individual can sacrificially love and regularly forgive others, thus demonstrating an unconditional commitment to another's well-being. In **John 13:34-35**, Jesus taught, **"I give you a new command: Love one another. Just as I have loved you, you are also to love one another. By this everyone will know that you are My disciples, if you love one another."** Similar to the unnamed woman in this biblical story, who was loved, forgiven, saved, and then directed by her Savior in **Luke 7:50** to **"Go in peace,"** we too can release our sinful past, surrender our current struggles, and entrust our future concerns into the faithful hands of the heavenly Father. We also can trust Christ by faith, receive His gift of mercy, and go forward in peace, changed by the gospel message and mission of the compassionate Messiah.

With the conclusion of this beloved woman's story, I can't help but wonder what she did after she left the host's home that evening in peace, assured of Christ's love and forgiveness? Did she run and tell others around the town about her glorious encounter with the merciful

Savior, even in her disheveled tear-stained, oil-soaked state? Did she head back home in humbled silence and ponder all that had just taken place? Perhaps she moved with urgency to the home of nearby relatives to share her experience of the gift of salvation received that outweighed the cost of her outpoured ointment or the need to wash her oily hair. What would assurance of Christ's love, forgiveness, and peace spur you to do next?

For those of us who recognize and appreciate how much we are loved and forgiven by the Savior, manifested through His finished sacrificial work on the cross and glorious resurrection, it seems fitting that we would respond by loving others more and hating others less, and forgiving others more and holding fewer grudges. This is a completely challenging response, and may even appear impossible, which is why we need to rely on Jesus and cling to His Word. May we consistently pray for God to enable us to love and forgive as He does, so that we may better represent the Savior whom we serve as His faithful ambassadors.

A thankful heart and attitude of gratitude can encourage us to forgive others and love more deeply. This further demonstrates our submission to the Savior by living at peace with others, even when faced with challenging circumstances (**Romans 12:18**). Let's serve others well when presented with opportunities to love sacrificially and forgive intentionally; let's not hesitate to cry out to the Lord for help when we falter in either case. He sees, He knows, He understands, and He cares about you.

**Application Acrostic**

**L**ook to Jesus first

**O**bey God's Word

**V**alue the lives of others

**E**xhibit compassion generously

**S**erve another's needs tangibly

**Thinking Through This**

- Recall when the depth of love you had for someone else became apparent to you. How did you demonstrate that love? What was your motivation?
- When have you experienced a season when it was difficult to love or forgive another person? How did you handle that relationship?
- What do you appreciate most about the love and forgiveness God has shown toward you?
- Who can you directly serve this week by taking the opportunity to generously express compassion for their needs?

**Further Findings of God's Mercy**

Read **Matthew 18:23-35** to study the parable of a *nameless but known* unforgiving servant and a compassionate master before the throne.

# Chapter 6

## THE DISABLED WOMAN IN THE SYNAGOGUE

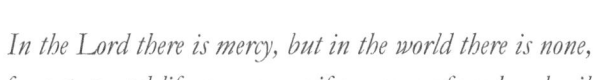

*In the Lord there is mercy, but in the world there is none,
for nature and life move on as if unaware of good and evil,
of human sorrow or human pain.*

My husband and I have two adult sons who are two years apart in age. Our family has experienced a wild ride over the past two decades, raising and nurturing two sons who function at different levels on the intellectual spectrum. This, in turn, has affected our children's academics, capabilities, communication styles, interpersonal relationships, responses to their environments, and their outlooks on life.

As of the time of writing this book, my youngest son has lived for 18 years with an incurable neurological disorder. This means our parenting responsibility for him has transformed into a court-appointed caregiver role. Our disabled son has endured years of countless and costly doctors' visits, therapy sessions, special education courses, nutritional programs, alongside other valuable resources to aid in his physical and psychological development. More importantly, God has provided for our son's spiritual-growth needs through the involvement and partnership we maintain with a local church body. The Lord has graciously and patiently tended to the hearts, minds, and souls of both our sons as they have been included and involved in various ministries within our church family, beginning and continuing with hearing and learning the gospel truth from God's Word. In both the home and the church, each son has been encouraged to know, love, and follow Jesus, even though their faith journeys in their understanding and practice of the things of God differ because of their differences in intellectual abilities.

We know and believe that God created both our sons as fearfully and wonderfully made, with purpose in mind for His glory, regardless that one has a physical design that includes disability (**Psalm 139:13-16**). Though our son did not choose to have a neurological disorder, our family can choose our response to the diagnosis. One of the most freeing aspects as a parent navigating this complex trek of our child's physical limitations is the recognition that the sovereign Creator takes responsibility for disability. This does not suggest that it's easy to accept that God's divine will may include *not* healing our child in the here and now, but rather the Lord empowers us to persevere through the ongoing challenges our son's current physical state includes. In **Exodus 4:11-12**, the Lord said to His servant, Moses, who dealt with a speech disability, **"Who placed a mouth on humans? Who makes a person mute or deaf, seeing or blind? Is it not I, the Lord? Now go! I will help you speak, and I will teach you what to say."**

If God has called you to compassionately care for one who lives with disability, then He will faithfully equip you to carry out this vital role, despite its share of daily demands and difficulties. Or if you live with a chronic disability yourself, then the sufficient Lord can provide what is needed for you to endure the hardship. May you seek to serve Christ in the physiological state in which you live, even if it encompasses limitations. Thankfully, a human being's disability does not restrict God from connecting spiritually with them. He calls them to serve and follow Him, even when that person believes they are hindered by their physical make-up. In addition, a disabled individual is *not* in any way less than an able-bodied person, though differently designed; both are priceless image-bearers of their merciful Creator (**Genesis 1:27**). Still, one person may face greater obstacles than the other, and need additional assistance throughout their lifetime, as they seek to honor their Savior. **Isaiah 64:8** explains, **"Yet Lord, You are our Father; we are the clay, and You are our Potter; we all are the work of Your hands."** Furthermore, **Ephesians 2:8-10** reminds us, **"For you are saved by grace through faith, and this is not from yourselves, it is God's gift – not from works, so that no one can boast. For we are His workmanship, created in Christ Jesus for good works, which God prepared ahead of time for us to do."**

As a parent of a child who lives with disability, I find myself thinking through some tough questions, like:

- Are we pointing our son to Jesus by encouraging him to rely on God's Word and helping him understand what it means to trust Christ in every area of life?
- Do we pray for our son's spiritual development with the same tenacity that we pray for his physical healing?
- Are we willing to entrust our son's life into our faithful Father's hands, whether our child's affliction remains or is cured?

Reflecting on these questions, I am reminded of the necessity to be connected to a local body of believers, since we need the support of the congregation. The church body has a wonderful opportunity to patiently minister to and intentionally include those with "special needs". This may not be an easy, convenient, or inexpensive undertaking, but it rightly models the compassion and mercy of the Creator God. At times, a church family may inadvertently impede those who live with disability from feeling welcomed, accepted, or even useful within the church body. Therefore, a church family may need to evaluate their responses to tough questions too. For example:

- Are we deliberate in providing opportunities for a disabled individual to participate, serve, and contribute within a church ministry?
- Do we offer a welcoming environment that is caring and includes those living with limitations?
- Are we willing to serve alongside disabled persons and support them on their faith journey, while remaining open to learning valuable lessons from them, too?

The Apostle Paul wrote of the beauty of the collective, diverse, redeemed members that form and unite the church family in **1 Corinthians 12:22-26: "…those parts of the body that are weaker are indispensable. And those parts of the body that we consider less honorable, we clothe these with greater honor…God has put the body together, giving greater honor to the less honorable, so that there would be no division in the body, but that the members would have the same concern for each other. So if one member suffers, all the members suffer with it; if one member is honored, all the members rejoice with it."**

My family and I have attempted to remain open for God to publicly use our special needs story to benefit others, specifically within the church setting. Truth be told, disability has not reduced or weakened our ministry. On the contrary, the Lord has expanded and enriched our mission in reaching other similar families for Jesus utilizing the platform of disability. Nevertheless, I must admit there have been brief, but painful seasons when I have temporarily allowed my son's disorder to hinder me from actively engaging within the church body. I cannot rationalize my reasons, for this cannot be rationalized; I can only confess that my coping skills fall short when personal insecurity rears its ugly head.

Perhaps you can understand what it's like to sometimes battle with self-inflicted shame or guilt, or to fight against periodic anxiety linked to understandable fears. Like me, maybe you struggle to stay afloat amid the ebb and flow of suppressed sorrow. Occasionally I grow weary of the recurrent responsibilities that are necessary to adequately care for an emerging disabled adult son, even though I am truly grateful to be his chosen mom. Often, I get tired of publicly dealing with bouts of momentary dissatisfaction with God's purposeful plan for my youngest son's physical design. This personal spiritual warfare creates a type of restricted bondage, from which I need to be repeatedly freed. I deeply desire to worship God with gratitude while trusting Him with the uncertain complexities of life. I am grateful for the indwelling Holy Spirit's power and the firm foundation of God's Word when I wrestle with doubts and lack understanding. **Romans 8:39** declares that there is nothing—not even disability — that can separate me or my son from the love of God in Christ Jesus our Lord.

Each of us will always need Jesus and His Word, no matter what we face on any given day. The divine Creator and Sustainer of the world chooses to heal some from their physical affliction and permits others to remain in their infirmity, yet we all need God's matchless mercy. Thankfully, God's Son has the authority to spiritually redeem any individual He chooses by grace through faith in Him. Jesus is the One who strengthens and sustains us throughout our temporary existence on earth regardless of the burdens we bear. This includes a nameless but known DISABLED WOMAN IN THE SYNAGOGUE whose biblical story is chronicled in **Luke 13:10-17**.

> **¹⁰ As He was teaching in one of the synagogues on the Sabbath, ¹¹ a woman was there who had been disabled by a spirit for over eighteen years. She was bent over and could not straighten up at all. ¹² When Jesus saw her, He called out to her, 'Woman, you are free of your disability.' ¹³ Then He laid His hands on her, and instantly she was**

restored and began to glorify God. ¹⁴ But the leader of the synagogue, indignant because Jesus had healed on the Sabbath, responded by telling the crowd, 'There are six days when work should be done; therefore come on those days and be healed and not on the Sabbath day.' ¹⁵ But the Lord answered him and said, 'Hypocrites! Doesn't each one of you untie his ox or donkey from the feeding trough on the Sabbath and lead it to water? ¹⁶ Satan has bound this woman, a daughter of Abraham, for eighteen years—shouldn't she be untied from this bondage on the Sabbath day?' ¹⁷ When He had said these things, all His adversaries were humiliated, but the whole crowd was rejoicing over all the glorious things He was doing.

Upon reading this scriptural story, we learn of an encounter between Jesus and a woman who lived with long-term disability. Though the narrative only takes eight verses within one biblical chapter, it offers multiple lessons about the demonstration of God's mercy. At first glance, it seems like this woman's meeting with Jesus was for the primary purpose of healing her from her physical infirmity. Though that was an observable result, in further examining the text, we learn the woman's bodily weakness was the platform Christ utilized to publicly reveal His compassionate concern for an individual's spiritual bondage. We learn from this biblical passage that for those living in bondage, true freedom comes from trusting in Jesus, who has the power to deliver today and for eternity. **"I am the Lord your God…I broke the bars of your yoke and enabled you to live in freedom" (Leviticus 26:13).**

In his devotional book, *Sunday Matters*©, author Paul David Tripp offers this inspirational prayer to the heavenly Father: "When I am burdened, You are my helper. I have come to understand that I should not fear weakness. My weakness is a workroom for Your grace. Your plan is for me to be a broken vessel so Your power gets attention, so

You are celebrated, so You are worshiped, so You get praise and not me. So, I will never give up. I will not lose heart."[10]

The Apostle Paul understood this outlook when he penned **2 Corinthians 12:9** after pleading with the Lord multiple times to remove his tormenting "thorn in the flesh" for which the Lord replied, **"My grace is sufficient for you, for My power is perfected in weakness."** What a helpful perspective on human weakness and a reminder that our brokenness is for the glory of God to point others to the power of Jesus. May our study of God's Word in Luke 13 encourage you today, whatever you may be enduring.

The nameless but known disabled woman's story can be broken into four parts: (1) the *place* of the encounter; (2) the *persons* involved within this gathering; (3) the *problem* Jesus addressed, and (4) the *purpose* of God's mercy displayed.

## The Place

As a recognized Jewish Rabbi, Jesus was found teaching in a local synagogue within the Judean region when He noticed the disabled woman among the crowd. A synagogue was a common place of worship for a Jewish assembly and primarily existed as a location for the instruction of the Old Testament Scriptures. A synagogue had an appointed religious ruler who managed the building, oversaw the service agenda, gave approval for the local rabbi to teach, and lastly, would participate in the gathering along with his assigned helpers.

As was His habit, Jesus often taught in the synagogue on the Sabbath, but He was not limited to that one holy day to preach a sermon. The detail about the Sabbath Day provided in Luke 13 is significant because Jesus was often falsely charged by the local religious leaders of failing to comply with the Sabbath law. This frequently stirred up conflict with Jesus' accusers. Their allegations became more

---

[10] Paul David Tripp, *Sunday Matters: 52 Devotionals to Prepare Your Heart for Church* (Wheaton, IL: Crossway, 2023), 127-128.

pronounced when the religiously elite amped up their efforts to trick and trap Jesus in His words or actions. They diligently sought to find a warrant to arrest Him for wrongdoing to silence Him, but their man-made plan was divinely prevented. Perhaps they felt threatened by Him and His gospel message, or jealous of the people's strong interest in Him. Jesus was known for preaching a sermon of forgiveness and redemption with an invitation for all people. Anyone who would repent, place their faith in Jesus as Savior, and believe His Word would be granted eternal life and included in God's Kingdom. What the misinformed religious leaders failed to understand was that Jesus Christ is Lord of the Sabbath and came to fulfill the very Law the devout rulers sought to uphold (**Luke 6:5**).

The Sabbath Day of rest was instituted by God Himself prior to the sinful fall of mankind; however, depraved humanity had turned the Lord's holy day of rest into some type of legalistic mandate that subtly distracted people from drawing near to the divine Messiah and His Word. Resting from work is not designed to nullify enacting deeds of mercy and kindness toward another, especially when one is afforded an opportunity to care for the immediate needs of a suffering person, even when tradition is at stake.

Scripture records a different Sabbath occasion in Luke 6 when Jesus was teaching in the synagogue. With the same tactic, the scribes and Pharisees closely watched Jesus to observe if He would heal another person so they could bring a charge against Him. The Bible notes that Jesus knew their thoughts, meaning He understood the ulterior motive behind their plan. So, Jesus asked this religious group a pertinent question prior to restoring a crippled man who was present, **"Is it lawful to do good on the Sabbath or to do evil, to save life or to destroy it?" (Luke 6:9).** Though momentarily silenced, the religious leaders were filled with rage by this question and bothered by the Messiah's subsequent compassion demonstrated toward a grateful individual. Rather than praise God for His gift of restoration, they discussed amongst themselves a way to get rid of the troublemaker.

Giving grace or extending mercy should not be viewed as an inconvenient act of manual labor; rather, it is a tangible expression of honoring the Lord as we seek to serve others.

The woman with the long-term disability was not the only person within this synagogue who was dealing with personal bondage, but her captivity was visible to the congregation, versus those enslaved to their concealed sinful attitude toward Jesus. In **1 Samuel 16:7**, the prophet mistakenly focused on a person's outward appearance in determining leadership capability, yet he rightly sought the Lord for wisdom. Then the Lord cautioned the prophet and said, **"Humans do not see what the Lord sees, for humans see what is visible, but the Lord sees the heart."** We are reminded that the sovereign Creator sees things differently than does fallen mankind. He often operates contrary to what we expect for His glory, and to make His name and purpose known among multiple peoples. Even today, in our generation, we struggle with focusing on the outward appearance within a public setting. Not surprisingly, living in bondage can take on various forms, but genuine freedom begins with trusting in Christ and His Word. He has the power to deliver from temporary or eternal captivity and break the chains of confinement, no matter the place.

## The Persons

Now that we have peered into the place of the encounter between Jesus and the disabled woman, let's become familiar with the persons involved in this memorable gathering. First, we recognize the *divine Teacher*, Jesus the Son of God. He was keenly aware of all the persons present among the crowd and chose to call out one solitary female. Jesus saw this woman in her current physical state, even if she could not raise her eyes to glimpse the Teacher because of her physical bondage. Though bent over, she could certainly hear the kind voice speaking to her. The unknown woman did not have to see to believe and obey the Savior's call for her to come into His presence (**John 20:29**).

Jesus had the authority to preach the Word of God, the power to cure an incurable disorder, and the foreknowledge of the cause for this woman's impairment. On this Sabbath Day, in a typical synagogue setting, Jesus chose to display an unexpected miracle of mercy, and drove home a deeper message. The divine Teacher addressed the danger of spiritual depravity that extended beyond the confines of healing a physical disability. Not only did the Messiah call a suffering woman to Himself, but He also called out His adversaries by questioning their callous and devious intentions and affirmed His sovereignty over both the physical and the spiritual realms.

The divine Teacher was not the only one present within that place, but secondly, we notice the *disabled woman*. What details are given about this handicapped woman? She is referred to by Jesus as a "daughter of Abraham." This biblical term could refer to her spiritual standing as a child of God, her ancestral heritage as a Jewish-bred woman, or indicate both. Because she was included within the congregation, as opposed to being shunned, she was not considered unclean by her 18-year-long disability. During that extended time, this woman was not able to straighten her upper body, which likely meant she had undergone a progressive decline in her physical stature.

Within the Mosaic Law, physical disability is addressed in **Levitus 21:16-23** and references various types of bodily deformities called "defects" that includes a condition labeled *hunchback*. Hunchback was deemed a physical condition that resulted from injuries to the spine. This defect often afflicted young girls who typically carried heavy loads on their shoulders or hips. Those within the congregation probably assumed that this was the cause of this woman's disability, with no known cure.[11] Her physical syndrome would have carried a social stigma like those inflicted with a chronic illness or long-term disease. It was often presumed during biblical times that disability was the

---

[11] Trent C. Butler, editor, *Holman Concise Bible Dictionary* (Nashville, TN: Broadman & Holman Publishers, 2001), 167-169.

consequence of personal or parental sin (**John 9:1-2**), or people assumed an individual was inflicted by a curse of an enemy (**Mark 9:20-21**).

Our Luke 13 passage notes the actual cause for this nameless woman's disability—she had been bound or tied up by an evil disabling spirit, originated by Satan, but permitted by God. This limitation was an oppressive influence *within* her life, rather than a force of possession *of* her life. A spiritually redeemed person cannot be possessed by Satan or his demons, but can certainly be oppressed and afflicted by the enemy, as **Job 1-2** in the Bible illustrates. Effective healing remedies were rare within the 1$^{st}$ Century, which is why so many people with physical ailments flocked to Jesus. He demonstrated on more than one occasion that He had the power to heal people from their physical captivity and deliver them from oppressive spiritual bondage. The disabled woman might not have shown up to the synagogue service for the purpose of physical healing the day she encountered Jesus, but it's notable that she did not allow her deformity to hinder her from gathering with her church family.

The Bible does not reveal the disabled woman's age, marital status, or if she had children. It's unclear if someone cared for her physically or provided for her financially. We also don't know how often and intensely she previously prayed for deliverance from bondage, or if she sought help for healing from traditional methods. Did she use all her money to seek out a cure, only to end up bankrupt and physically worse off? What we know is that Jesus saw a disabled woman in the worship service, stopped His sermon, and called out to her. She immediately obeyed the Savior's voice without questioning Him or doubting His declaration of freedom from her captivity.

By His rightful choice, Jesus healed this unnamed crippled woman by His merciful words and powerful touch; He freed her immediately and completely from her oppressive, debilitating bondage. The woman's physical state was changed that day, within a worship service no less. In addition, this newly-cured female's spiritual state was impacted, as evidenced in her swift praising the Lord, glorifying Him for her transformed stature. By the time this remarkable scenario wrapped up, a liberated woman was not the only person rejoicing for all the glorious things done by the heavenly Healer.

Regrettably, not everyone present within this sacred gathering on the Sabbath in the synagogue was delighted by this meeting disturbance. Third, we observe a person depicted as the *displeased ruler* in the Luke 13 narrative. He was an annoyed spiritual leader who appeared more concerned with the ritualistic scheduled ceremony than with caring for a suffering sister in his congregation. Evidently, this chief leader had a bone to pick with Jesus, whom the leader mistook for "working" on the Sabbath, thus breaking the sacred commandment. According to traditional guidelines, a professional physician was considered working if treating a person's ailment on a Sabbath Day. Rather than directly confronting Jesus, this displeased ruler indirectly issued a verbal warning to the crowd. In this irked ruler's likely attempt to publicly reprimand Jesus and insult His intelligence in matters of the Law, the Son of God did not hesitate to address him. Jesus would not tolerate hypocrisy from His adversaries in this celebratory moment. They failed to connect with the very Savior whom they needed themselves to free them from their bondage of self-righteousness.

If all we can do is find ways to criticize, complain, and find fault with the work of the Lord, particularly within a church setting, then we may need to reevaluate our understanding of the gospel message of Christ and the purpose of the church. Is there something inhibiting you from expressing gratitude for the Lord's mighty deeds? Is there anything keeping you from celebrating with others when God provides deliverance for them? Are you actively participating in the work of God that involves compassionately caring for other church members? I freely admit that it is necessary for me to conduct a personal heart-check more often than not, especially within a church gathering, to see if I might be deterring my own spiritual progress, or hindering some else's, by a sour attitude or critical spirit. How about you?

Jesus' corrective response to the displeased ruler was necessary within the synagogue setting. The religious party often did more damage issuing paralyzing regulations linked to the Sabbath, inadvertently causing it to feel like one of the most burdensome days of the week for congregants. Instead, those in attendance should have been encouraged to freely worship the Lord God and celebrate His goodness for salvation through Christ.

A divine Teacher, a disabled woman, and a displeased ruler were not the only persons in attendance during this chronicled meeting with Jesus. Finally, we see the *disconcerted crowd*. The local congregants probably dealt with confusion about whether they should respond with celebration or be subject to condemnation. They might have felt uncertain whether they would be found guilty by association or be rewarded with blessing based on their reaction to the encounter. The disconcerted crowd was privy to the teaching of God's Word and observed all that took place. Maybe some of those present had their own hidden afflictions, were in need of remedy, and searching for hope. Perhaps others were ready to experience freedom as well, but felt fearful of what others would say if their private bondage was exposed.

The synagogue attendees had a choice to make of how they would respond to the divine Teacher, to the disabled woman, and even to the demands of the displeased ruler. Would the multitude choose to celebrate or criticize the work of the Lord? For those living in bondage, would they choose to trust Jesus and His power to deliver them? What if their request to God echoed **Psalm 142:7, "Free me from prison so that I can praise Your name"**? No matter the countless reactions that happened during the unidentified woman's meeting with Jesus, in a public place allocated to bringing a diverse group of people together, a problem or two was bound to arise.

**The Problem**

Some of the initial physical and relational problems exposed in Luke 13 were previously addressed within this chapter, but there is a deeper spiritual problem that is the focus within this nameless but known woman's story. Every human being is born with a sin problem that can only be remedied by Jesus Christ. Our depraved state of captivity produces a desperate need for the Savior to liberate us and restore us to a right relationship with our Creator.

God the Father has made a way for a repentant sinner to be redeemed and delivered from oppressive bondage of sin and death through His Son's final sacrificial work on the cross. Jesus' resurrection from the grave confirmed that secured eternal life is possible. Similar to the participants present in the synagogue, church attendees today struggle with affliction and bondage, perhaps even lacking compassion for those suffering worse than others. We battle with surrendering our will to the Lord, our desires, our preferences, and we struggle with entrusting our hardship to Him. We further resist releasing *false* control to God for our difficult situation, which hinders us from resting in God's proven faithfulness. Let's return to God's Word regularly to remember Who He is and what He has done. May we trust God to continue to do a purposeful work within each of us as we cooperate with the work of the indwelling Holy Spirit. **First Peter 5:10 proclaims, "The God of all grace, who called you to His eternal glory in Christ, will Himself restore, establish, strengthen, and support you after you have suffered a little while."**

One of the problems with recurring bondage is that it frequently causes us to concentrate more on our circumstances or issues than stay focused on Christ, who can free us from bondage. Even if the Lord does not afford immediate relief from our persistent pain, we can trust that He will provide what is necessary for us to endure by renewing our strength. One of the supportive ways God provides for those dealing with a discouraging season of bondage is the availability of the church body to encourage and pray for one another. Instead of immediately offering advice on how another person should fix their problem, perhaps we simply begin with expressing empathy and offer a calming presence, so they realize they are not facing their burden alone. **James 5:13, 16** asks, **"Is anyone among you suffering? He should pray…pray for one another, so that you may be healed. The prayer of a righteous person is very powerful in its effect."**

For a Christ-follower, prayer should be the default response to a problem—we take it to God. We might not receive an instant answer or understand the purpose when our pain continues, though all suffering is meant to draw us nearer to God. Let us release our unbearable problem to the One who is able to do the impossible, if He so chooses. This prayerful response just might be what leads us to freely praise the Lord, even when we ache or are ailing deeply.

## The Purpose

During this study of Luke 13, we explored the place of the encounter, learned about the people involved, and discussed the problem addressed. We conclude by considering the purpose of God's mercy displayed.

In demonstration of God's matchless mercy, and through His limitless power to deliver, Jesus gave the gift of freedom from a lasting heavy burden to an unassuming individual. Jesus spoke within the biblical text that it was necessary for this daughter of Abraham to be loosed from her debilitating bondage. It was time to be freed, no longer restrained by the enemy, but unchained from the oppressive burden on her back. Jesus acknowledged the woman's value as a created image-bearer of her Creator over and above a prized animal, like an ox or a donkey. This disabled female encountered the compassion of Jesus, and He literally straightened her out. **John 8:36** declares, **"So if the Son sets you free, you really will be free."** The liberated woman's immediate response to her newfound freedom was to praise the Lord God, perhaps with her head, arms, and voice lifted high—perhaps for the first time in 18 years—to the only One worthy of all praise and glory.

God uses our brokenness to display His grace and reveals His miracle of mercy through salvation in Christ. Jesus spoke boldly about meaningful purpose within infirmity, so that God's works may be displayed within the disabled individual (**John 9:3**). The Lord continues to use emotional, physical, relational or spiritual bondage to display His redemptive work. By His matchless mercy, He has the power to change lives or circumstances for His glory. **Psalm 138:8** comforts the weary soul, **"The Lord will fulfill His purpose for me. Lord, Your faithful love endures forever; do not abandon the work of Your hands."** Though you may not be confined by a physical disability, perhaps you are experiencing a form of bondage from your inability to forgive another who has hurt you; or enslaved to a harmful addiction to cope with your suffering; or held captive by your fears of the uncertain future; or feel crushed by the weight of your past mistakes. Perhaps you are experiencing a paralyzing effect from daily grief because of tragic loss. May you be drawn into the presence of God and captured by His comforting Word, for He is a God who restores in due time for His redeeming purpose.

The Lord is faithful to meet you right where you are in your affliction. His grace is sufficient, His mercy is matchless, His power is made perfect in weakness, so continue to celebrate your glorious freedom found in Christ. **"For I consider that the sufferings of this present time are not worth comparing with the glory that is going to be revealed to us…For the creation was subjected to futility – not willingly…that the creation itself will also be set free from the bondage to decay into the glorious freedom of God's children" (Romans 8:18, 20-21).**

**Application Acrostic**

**F**ear not your affliction

**R**est in God's faithfulness

**E**ntrust your affliction to God

**E**xpress praise for God's provision

**Thinking Through This**

- What are some possible causes of bondage for individuals?
- What are plausible ways individuals may seek deliverance from their bondage?
- Why do non-disabled people often struggle with relating to those who live with disability?
- How might you celebrate your spiritual freedom in Christ, even if experiencing a chronic or recurring physical affliction?

**Further Findings of God's Mercy**

To study the story of a *nameless but known* woman near the sea, inflicted with a blood disorder, read the similar passages of **Matthew 9:18-22; Mark 5:21-34;** and **Luke 8:40-48**.

# Chapter 7

## THE WIDOWED WOMAN OUTSIDE THE CITY

*Mercy is an attribute of God, an infinite and inexhaustible energy within the divine nature that disposes God to be actively compassionate.*

One Sunday morning, my husband, who is a pastor on staff at our local church, was scheduled to preach the message during the worship service. He had delivered the biblical sermon twice that morning before I entered the worship center to participate in the third gathering. Prior to the start of the service, I was sitting in a back pew of the sanctuary chatting with another woman when I noticed my husband walking toward me. He sat down in the pew in front of me, and I sensed something was wrong, since he rarely leaves the front of the sanctuary before preaching to come speak to me in the middle of a Sunday morning. But that morning was unique because of a tragedy that happened the previous night to a church family, who was then unexpectedly present during the pending church service.

In a hushed tone, my husband quickly informed me that one of our seasoned church members, a 64-year-old devoted husband and dad, had died suddenly and silently from a heart attack at his home the night before. I was shocked and had no words to say, other than asking my husband if he was absolutely sure about this heartbreaking news. We had spent time with this man and his wife on more than one occasion because my oldest son and their youngest son attended the same high school, graduated in the same class, and played sports together. After my husband delivered the sad news to me, he mentioned that this deceased man's freshly widowed wife, hours after her husband's death, was seated alongside her immediate family within this third worship service. Remarkably, they chose to gather with their church family to worship their faithful Lord and risen Savior amid their real and raw grief. It was an astonishing testimony of courageous faith that, upon the death of this beloved husband, his sorrowful wife chose to incorporate her church family within a public setting as a starting point for her unwelcomed season of mourning.

My husband pointed out where this widowed mother was sitting within the sanctuary, so I quickly rose from my seat and made a beeline for her. All I could offer her in that sorrowful moment was my brief presence accompanied by a compassionate hug and a few shallow words of condolence. Her plight weighed heavily on my mind throughout the following week leading up to her husband's memorial service. I prayed for her family and the necessary decisions to be made in days and weeks to come, since her husband managed his own business and was the primary breadwinner for his household.

I was not able to attend the funeral for this widow's husband due to a prior ministry event scheduled the same day, at a similar time, at the same location, but in a different building. However, I was able to slip over to the sanctuary at the end of the memorial service once my event had concluded. I considered the irony that one church event included participants celebrating while another event nearby included participants mourning. Two different crowds meeting up with each other on the same date, but for different purposes; yet the Lord God was sovereign over both events. Within both settings, God's redeemed people praised Him for His goodness.

The Lord provided me with a private opportunity that afternoon to speak briefly with the widowed mother before we went our separate ways. After I hugged her and further expressed my sadness for her loss, I told her that she was an inspiration to me with her astonishing choice the week prior to attend the Sunday worship service the day after her husband's passing. Observing her response to that personal tragedy caused me to assess whether I could have been that brave and committed to attend a church gathering, should the tables have been turned. Without hesitation, this godly widow replied to me, "I had to come; there was no place else I wanted to be." Could the same sentiment be said of you and me? Amid sorrow or rejoicing, when Jesus Christ is the focus, is there any other place we would want to be than hope-filled and gloriously worshipping the only One worthy of praise and honor with our church family?

**First Thessalonians 4:13-14** encourages believers, **"We do not want you to be uninformed, brothers and sisters, concerning those who are asleep so that you will not grieve like the rest, who have no hope. For if we believe that Jesus died and rose again, in the same way, through Jesus, God will bring with Him those who have fallen asleep."** The reference to those who are asleep implies deceased Christ-followers. These verses remind us that for the redeemed family of God, members can grieve with hope because of the reality of the risen Savior. Furthermore, in **Ecclesiastes 7:14**, the Bible exhorts, **"In the day of prosperity, be joyful, but in the day of adversity, consider: God has made the one as well as the other, so that no one can discover anything that will come after him."** In addition, **Ecclesiastes 3:14** explains that God works in such a way that people will be in awe of Him. We trust God for today and we continue to trust Him for tomorrow. We believe in and rely on His holy Word, whatever the day may bring. Meanwhile, whether facing hardship or ease, we continue to gather weekly with His church bride to be reminded of the sovereign God's goodness through the risen

Savior, Jesus Christ, and we continue to proclaim the hope-filled gospel message of salvation.

We were never meant to carry our burdens alone. **Galatians 6:2** exhorts the church members to, **"Carry one another's burdens, in this way you will fulfill the law of Christ."** Likewise, **1 Peter 5:7** encourages the church family, who will endure burdens, to respond to God by, **"Casting all your cares on Him, because He cares about you."** Bearing another's burdens can be tiresome, and releasing your burdens into God's hands can feel terrifying. Nevertheless, both actions are worthwhile investments in caring with compassion in action for one another, while entrusting the situation to the divine Caregiver. In his book, *Sunday Matters*©, the author provides this insightful commentary:

> God has designed for us to gather with one another again and again precisely because we are weak and needy people who were not designed for independent living. As we gather, we remember again that there is One who cares for us and who is both willing and capable of meeting us in our moment of burden and doing in us and for us what no one else would be able to do. We gather to remember that our Lord understands what we are going through, because for 33 years He walked in our shoes, experiencing all the burdens we now experience…He rules all the situations and locations where we carry those anxieties, burdens, and cares. He is present with us always, promising to never leave or forsake us. His grace is inexhaustible, His love is boundless, and his mercies are new every morning.[12]

The presence and provision of Jesus were a welcomed change for a nameless but known WIDOWED WOMAN OUTSIDE THE CITY who was carrying a heavy burden when she unexpectedly met the Savior

---

[12] Paul David Tripp, *Sunday Matters: 52 Devotionals to Prepare Your Heart for Church* (Wheaton, IL: Crossway, 2023), 116.

traveling with an entourage. Her biblical story is recorded in **Luke 7:11-17**.

> **¹¹ Afterward He was on His way to a town called Nain. His disciples and a large crowd were traveling with Him. ¹² Just as He neared the gate of the town, a dead man was being carried out. He was his mother's only son, and she was a widow. A large crowd from the town was also with her. ¹³ When the Lord saw her, He had compassion on her and said, 'Don't weep.' ¹⁴ Then He came up and touched the open coffin, and the pallbearers stopped. And He said, 'Young man, I tell you, get up!' ¹⁵ The dead man sat up and began to speak, and Jesus gave him to his mother. ¹⁶ Then fear came over everyone, and they glorified God, saying, 'A great Prophet has risen among us,' and 'God has visited His people.' ¹⁷ This report about Him went throughout Judea and all the vicinity.**

This passage of Scripture illustrates a sobering, exceptional day in the life of a widowed mother from a small, insignificant town called Nain. She encountered the beloved Son of God, who has the power to bring hope to any tragedy by His matchless mercy. We only have seven biblical verses that tell this nameless woman's story, yet they provide great insight into the compassion and power of Jesus Christ. He purposefully met this sorrowful woman in a public setting where more than one crowd witnessed this divinely orchestrated scene.

Our biblical text from Luke 7 offers four types of meetings included in this historical event. Each teaches us the value of a community gathering when it includes the Messiah and His mercy. First, there is a *<u>momentary meeting</u>* of a city crowd and a cemetery crowd.

**Luke 7:11** begins by stating, **"Afterward..."** and indicates that Jesus was not alone in traveling to Nain, but was accompanied by His original disciples along with a multitude. Where had this group just come from? If you were to glance at the scriptural story recorded prior to this journey to Nain, you would discover that Jesus had just performed a miracle while ministering in Capernaum, and healed a centurion's fatally ill servant. Capernaum was about 25 miles north of Nain in the region of Galilee, and it took about a day to travel on foot between the two towns. This Gentile official in Capernaum, known for his kindness towards the Jewish community, acknowledged Jesus' authority through his designated spokesman, and confessed his unworthiness to be in the physical presence of the Lord.

There are two references in the Bible which note that Jesus "marveled" or was "amazed" over something or someone (**Mark 6:6; Luke 7:9**). In this case, Christ marveled over the genuine faith of this Gentile leader, who had not been raised to follow the God of Israel. Yet this military commander believed that Jesus was so powerful and authoritative that He could just say the word from afar and the centurion's beloved servant would be healed immediately. Interestingly, Jesus did not utter a word of healing, but rather spoke of this prominent officer's faith in the Word of God. When those whom the centurion had sent to appeal to Jesus returned to the house where the dying servant lay, they found him physically well.

This is the celebratory event that happened just prior to Jesus— surrounded by a city crowd—making His way toward the next town. Perhaps the mass of people continued to follow where Jesus went in hopes of hearing additional teaching from the Messiah or to witness Him performing another miracle. Jesus was purposely and precisely leading this procession to the village of Nain, which means "pleasant," that overlooked the plain of Esdraelon in southwest Galilee. God's providence provided the opportunity for a joyful crowd to confront a sorrowful cemetery crowd with Jesus at the center of it all. At the center of the Nain funeral crowd on the way to the cemetery, though, was a grieving widowed mother and her deceased only son in an open coffin.

To offer some biblical background on a Jewish funeral procession, the deceased person was typically buried on the same day they died. Honoring the deceased individual was important in Jewish tradition. The relatives of the person who had passed away would follow the lifeless body lying flat in an open casket that looked like a type of stretcher, and was carried by four pallbearers, one at each corner. The family procession would make its way slowly through the town toward the graveyard while bystanders witnessed this somber parade. These onlookers would be expected to join the procession out of respect for the family of the deceased, especially when hired mourners drew attention to the funeral procession. Subsequently, the mourning process for the family members would continue for approximately 30 days. It would have been highly unlikely for Jesus and the city crowd to casually pass by this cemetery crowd without stopping and paying their respects, however, Jesus' plan encompassed something far greater than a spontaneous meeting between the two groups.

After the initial meeting took place, the Luke 7 story provides details of a second type of encounter, a *meaningful meeting* between the renowned Savior and the distressed widow. The well-known Messiah had foreknowledge of the unnamed distraught woman and her tragic plight as a now-childless widow with no prospect of having additional children, and now facing the interment of her only loved one. This mother was left helpless without adequate provision or financial resources for survival; her future looked bleak. The Bible describes that the Lord Jesus saw the woman, had overflowing compassion for her, and then spoke words of comfort to her during this glorious gathering wrapped in grief. It is noteworthy that two large crowds surrounded Jesus, as reports were spreading throughout the region of who Jesus was and what He could do on behalf of those with identifiable needs. Nevertheless, He zeroed in on one unnoticed hurting individual among the crowd; He made a deliberate point to exclusively address her on her most profound day of sorrow. Jesus saw the widowed mother and He stopped what He was doing to meet her in her mourning with His compassionate presence and comforting words, not to mention His miracle.

One definition of compassion is "your pain in my heart." It is to feel passion, pity, or devotion to someone in need, and to sympathetically enter their sorrow or pain by seeking a concrete expression of love.[13] Compassion typically occurs during distressing circumstances in an attempt to console the suffering person and care for them in their struggle. Jesus hurt deeply for this woman; He could identify with her heartache. **Isaiah 53:3** prophetically declared that Jesus understands sorrow as One who was acquainted with grief. He comprehends the pain that sin and death continually cause inhabitants residing in a broken and decaying world.

Jesus did not deny or diminish this widowed mother's struggle, but He knew He had the power to extend mercy toward her and change her dilemma for her good and the glory of God. Offering compassion to another does not need to be dictated by whether the needy person is or is not deserving of help; compassion in action is the timely choice to minister to the one in need during their moment of crisis. Kindheartedness should be a natural characteristic of believers, since it is an attribute that models the sacred Savior, whose example they are committed to follow. **Psalm 103:13** conveys, **"As a father has compassion on his children, so the Lord has compassion on those who fear Him."**

---

[13] Trent C. Butler, editor, *Holman Concise Bible Dictionary* (Nashville, TN: Broadman & Holman Publishers, 2001), 129.

Outside the village of Nain, Jesus was not afraid nor uncomfortable about confronting humanity's misery; He responded to a widowed mother's despair amid her cherished son's death. This devastated woman was so overwhelmed with grief that she did not even speak to Jesus, nor make a request of Him, perhaps because of her preoccupation with her loss. Possibly she was experiencing such a sense of hopelessness that she was all out of strength to utter even a feeble prayer. This does not suggest that this widow did not have faith in the purpose and plan of the Lord God of Israel. She needed others to intercede with prayer on her behalf and offer support during her season of mourning.

**Second Corinthians 1:3-4** offers insight into the biblical cycle of comfort, **"Blessed be the God and Father of our Lord Jesus Christ, the Father of mercies and the God of all comfort. He comforts us in all our affliction, so that we may be able to comfort those who are in any kind of affliction, through the comfort we ourselves receive from God."** Sharing in another's sufferings provides the pathway to share in their comfort too. This scriptural passage reminds us that for the redeemed family of God, we can grieve with hope because of the reality of the risen Savior.

No matter how active or busy we are, may we look up from our calendars, agendas, and tasks to notice other hurting people. May we be willing to stop, listen, respond with care and compassion, help where possible, pray for them, and make a point of being there to remind them they are not alone in their struggle. I'm reminded of a statement I heard that *others will not care how much we know until they know how much we care*. Similarly, author Walter Tubbs wrote these words: "If I do my thing and you do yours, we stand in danger of losing each other and ourselves...We are fully ourselves only in relation to each other...I do not find you by chance; I find you by an active life of reaching out."[14]

Lamentations 3 expresses the hopelessness that can occur when a person is facing affliction and no longer has the strength to endure. Still, the suffering person remembers the mercy of God and His powerful Word, thus bringing him or her hope beyond comprehension. The human author of **Lamentations 3:31-33** concludes, **"For the Lord will not reject us forever. Even if He causes suffering, He will show compassion according to the abundance of His faithful love. For He does not enjoy bringing affliction or suffering on mankind."**

When processing this meaningful meeting between the compassionate Savior who noticed the grieving widow and responded without delay to her plight, I recall a similar significant, but sorrowful moment in the life of a different grieving widowed mother who witnessed the death of her crucified beloved Son. This astonishing scene is presented in **John 19:26-27**, which reads, **"When Jesus saw His mother and the disciple He loved standing there, He said to His mother, 'Woman, here is your son.' Then He said to the disciple, 'Here is your mother.' And from that hour the disciple took her into his home."** During the crucial hours of shedding His blood for the forgiveness of sinful humanity, the dying incarnate Savior—divine Son of God, human Son of Mary—used some of His final words from the cross to extend overflowing compassion toward His own sorrowful mom. As the firstborn, Jesus desired to provide for His mother's future needs during that critical moment. Therefore, He called upon one of His faithful followers, John the treasured disciple, to further care for and support this cherished woman. [For further

---

[14] Charles R. Swindoll, and Walter Tubbs, "Beyond Pearls, Journal of Humanistic Psychology," *The Tale of the Tardy Oxcart and 1,501 Other Stories* (Nashville, TN: Word Publishing, 1998), 105.

study of Mary's story, pick up a copy of my book, *Odd Moms Out: God's redemptive grace in the lives of five biblical mothers*© (2022).]

Shortly after this final recorded discourse with His beloved mother, Jesus died and was buried, but the miracle of mercy was visually confirmed through Christ's subsequent resurrection from the grave. This signified the epitome of Jesus' victory over the enemy of death with the hope of eternal life for those who believe in Him. Similarly, Jesus went beyond simply noticing the widow from Nain to also providing for her needs; her only son lived on to provide for her well-being. How quickly do you and I demonstrate compassion in action toward another hurting individual to bring them hope? When have you benefited from another person extending compassion toward you during a pivotal time of need, thus bringing much welcomed comfort?

Luke 7 has presented a momentary meeting and a meaningful meeting, but this leads to third, a *miraculous meeting* involving the Savior and the only son of a widow. The Bible does not disclose details on the cause of the young man's death, but it is likely that he was the age of a teenager or emerging adult. The story mentions that Jesus came up to the bier – the casket – and touched it. The pallbearers carrying the open coffin immediately halted from moving forward to the burial site destination. It was at that moment that Jesus spoke to the nameless but known dead man with a majestic command for him to arise. In the blink of an eye, a former corpse was granted new life by the authoritative word of the only begotten Son of God. In addition, a new destination was established for this revived son; there was no further need to travel to the graveyard because he could return to his mother's household, reinstated with the respectable responsibility of caring for her and himself.

**First Peter 1:3** explains about God the Father, **"Because of His great mercy He has given us new birth into a living hope through the resurrection of Jesus Christ from the dead."** The evidence that an only son's life was restored was that he instantly sat up and began to speak. I wonder what the dead man, now raised to life, said as his first words upon his rebirth? Both crowds watching this spectacle were probably in shock. I cannot imagine how the widowed mother responded, other than with pure jubilation and her tears of sadness changed into tears of joy when Jesus gave this only son back to his grateful mom. Not only do we not know her name, but we have no recorded words spoken by her. Was she speechless, sobbing uncontrollably, so no words could be formed? Thankfully, she had witnesses from two crowds observing this miracle of new life or who would have believed her when she recounted the encounter? What a beautiful picture this story portrays of heavenly resurrection; the redeemed family of God only temporarily grieve with hope on earth by holding firmly to the reality of the risen Savior and eternal life in Christ. **Psalm 56:13** proclaims about the Lord, **"For You rescued me from death, even my feet from stumbling, to walk before God in the light of life."**

This phenomenal public moment of a miraculous meeting between the Savior and a deceased son illustrated without question that salvation and resurrection come only through Jesus Christ. I love that this Luke 7 story does not portray any objection by onlookers or confrontation by the religious leaders, as was often the case within other earlier *Nameless but Known* narratives. This was just an awe-inspiring miraculous meeting of the Savior, who was destined to die, facing a young son who was destined to live beyond what was originally expected by his family members and community.

Do you wonder, like I do, what that restored son did with his life after the incredible moment God's matchless mercy changed his reality? What personal testimony did he give of encountering the divine Redeemer and how He transformed his life? Did he impact his community by spreading the gospel message? Did the young man follow Jesus to the cross to view His death? Was he permitted to be an eyewitness of the risen Messiah prior to Jesus' ascension into heaven to be reunited with His Father? We don't know the answers to those questions; it is okay to have unknowns in the Bible. However, a question to consider by those of us who have been spiritually restored by the Savior is: *Are you and I living our daily lives to glorify God by testifying about Jesus, who has eternally changed our lives by His incomparable mercy?*

In **Galatians 2:20**, the Apostle Paul wrote, **"I have been crucified with Christ, and I no longer live, but Christ lives in me. The life I now live in the body, I live by faith in the Son of God, who loved me and gave Himself for me."** Jesus' purpose in performing this resurrection miracle went beyond benefitting one nameless widow and her unidentified son. This was a marvelous act that declared and demonstrated Christ's divine authority to grant eternal life beyond the grave of death. Jesus' birth, life, death, and resurrection have provided the hope-filled, secured assurance for the redeemed family of God to be brought together again one day with their risen Savior. If God has saved you, then you have been born again, raised to walk in new life as a new creation in Christ. In **Ephesians 4:1-3**, the Apostle Paul also urged born-again believers, **"…to walk worthy of the calling you have received, with all humility and gentleness, with patience, bearing with one another in love, making every effort to keep the unity of the Spirit through the bond of peace."** Does your redeemed life reflect a difference from your dead existence before your spiritual conversion, notably in the outward characteristics you exhibit?

As we finish our study of the nameless but known widowed woman outside the city, and reflect on a touching illustration of a glorious gathering amid grief, we conclude with the fourth and final converging of persons defined in Luke 7 with a *memorable meeting* of the Prophet and some of the onlookers and participants.

Evidently, fear seized the multitude, which implies a strong sense of awe overcame the people present during this memorable meeting. In turn, this spurred them to praise and glorify God. They rightly acknowledged Jesus as a Prophet who had arisen within their community; but true believers know He was and is so much more than that title. Christ continued to prove His divine nature and reveal His ultimate purpose for coming to the earth in human form.

If you continued reading in Luke 7, disciples of the imprisoned John the Baptist, Jesus' earthly distant cousin, told John about the miracle that happened for the widowed mother's deceased son. John sent these messengers back to Jesus to inquire and confirm if He was the true Messiah for whom Israel had been waiting. Jesus had previously been healing people of diseases, casting out evil spirits, restoring sight to the blind, but now He had raised a dead person to life. This was the remarkable report John received about Jesus, and what had been seen and heard. John, a faithful, but incarcerated disciple, was assured that the God-given mission work he had formerly accomplished to prepare the way for the Lord was indeed coming to fruition.

The participants praising God in **Luke 7:16** during this memorable meeting quoted, **"God has visited His people."** That statement had already been pronounced by the prophet Zechariah, John's dad, years prior to this recorded momentous event within Jesus' adult ministry. The celebratory message of God visiting His people was a prophecy of the coming newborn Messiah, now fulfilled here in the flesh. In **Luke 1:78-79**, Zechariah further declared, **"Because of our God's merciful compassion, the Dawn from on high will visit us to shine on those who live in darkness and the shadow of death, to guide our feet into the way of peace."**

Genuine peace comes from knowing Christ and His Word, embracing the hope of eternal life for those God has saved by grace through faith. One day, for the redeemed family of God, a glorious gathering will happen in heaven between Christ and His church bride when He comes again for her at the appointed time. The promise from the heavenly Father is that there will no longer be grief, pain, and suffering, nor death, but only permanent joy-filled everlasting life in the presence of our Living Hope. What a memorable meeting that will be!

On this side of eternity, we will not always understand the Lord's higher ways in the matters of life and death, but we can trust His Word that He is the originator of life and of death, regardless how one or the other occurs. Until we see Jesus face to face, let's maintain meeting with our church family and studying God's Word together. Whether members are experiencing a period of celebration or enduring a season of sorrow, we can spur one another to rejoice in God's matchless mercy. Since we can grieve with hope because of the marvelous reality of the risen Savior, we also must continue to encourage one another, as referenced in **Romans 15:13, "Now may the God of hope fill you with all joy and peace as you believe so that you may overflow with hope by the power of the Holy Spirit."**

### Application Acrostic

**H**elp carry someone else's burden

**O**ffer comfort to a person in despair

**P**ray for an individual who is grieving loss

**E**xplain the reason for your hope

## Thinking Through This

- How do you typically respond to a scenario that causes you to grieve deeply?
- What essential principle did you learn within this Luke 7 story? How does it help your outlook on your current circumstances?
- How might you express compassion in action for another person who is experiencing despair?
- What is the value of humility, gentleness, patience, and love when bearing with others in the context of a family household?

## Further Findings of God's Mercy

Read **1 Kings 17:8-24** to study the story of a different *nameless but known* widow and her son at the city gate.

# Conclusion

*We count on God's mercy for our past mistakes,
on God's love for our present needs, on God's sovereignty for our future.*
(Augustine of Hippo, bishop)

With the wrap-up of our biblical study of six nameless women who encountered the matchless mercy of God through the renowned Redeemer, I am grateful for the relevance of God's Word and the timeliness of scriptural insight provided by others' inspiring stories. Along the way, we have learned essential principles within each woman's story. We have identified with those who perhaps felt lost, alone, and unnoticed among the crowd, who struggled with hidden wounds and endured unfortunate situations. We have also been encouraged that these same women were noticed and known by the merciful Messiah and benefited from His demonstration of compassion in action as He met them in their misery and engaged in their struggles. Their life-changing stories chronicled in the Gospels point to the redeeming work of Jesus Christ, thus bringing renewed hope, and reminding us of the significance of embracing God's mercy and extending it to others. **Psalm 145:8-9** describes the prominence of God's marvelous mercy, **"The Lord is gracious and compassionate, slow to anger and great in faithful love. The Lord is good to everyone; His compassion rests on all He has made."**

Will you and I trust the God of the Bible and believe His Word even when our adverse situations prompt us to question God's goodness?

Throughout our journey, we have observed the various whereabouts of unnamed women from the past who were primarily known for their recurring struggles, repetitive sins, past mistakes, and challenging circumstances, but were nonetheless recognized by Jesus as those in desperate need of a Savior. They were each loved and cherished by the merciful Son of God, by His choice, who cared for each female's well-being during their prominent hour of need. **Romans 9:14-16** explains about God's mercy, **"I will show mercy to whom I will show mercy, and I will have compassion on whom I will have compassion. So then, it does not depend on human will or effort but on God who shows mercy."** None of the unidentified women could earn God's mercy by their own merit, and neither can we, but Christ's lovingkindness toward them demonstrated the matchless mercy of God shown to undeserving individuals. Only the Lord through Christ has the power to change lives, decisions, directions, or situations for the glory and purpose of God and the person's good, as God defines their good.

Perhaps you find yourself going along to get along with the crowd, but it has left you feeling unsatisfied. Possibly you have been unwisely coerced by societal influencers to act in opposition to the things of God, which sadly has left you to deal with a seared conscience, unwanted consequences, and broken dreams. Maybe the pain from your emotional or relational wounds is so deep that you don't see a way out of the darkness, and you have lost your way, not knowing who you can trust. **Proverbs 3:5-6** offers hope with helpful instruction, **"Trust in the Lord with all your heart, and do not rely on your own understanding; in all your ways know Him, and He will make your paths straight."** *Dear reader, do you know Christ as Lord and Savior?* God's Son is the singular way to be saved. He meets you where you are with open arms of compassion, no matter your location, circumstances or prior actions. Are you willing to come to Him in humbled surrender and call on His name to save you? Jesus' Name is the only name that counts for eternity.

Authors Charles R. Swindoll and J.I. Packer in their book, *Knowing God*©, effectively write: "What matters supremely, therefore, is not, in the last analysis, the fact that I know God, but the larger fact which underlies it – that He knows me…All my knowledge of Him depends on His sustained initiative in knowing me. I know Him because He first knew me, and continues to know me."[15]

**Acts 4:12** exclaims about Jesus Christ of Nazareth, **"There is salvation in no one else, for there is no other Name under heaven given to people by which we must be saved."** Furthermore, **John 15:16** confirms that those redeemed by God do not choose Jesus first, but in fact, Jesus is the One who chooses individuals out of the fallen world. He sets them apart as children of God to persevere by faith and remain devoted to Christ, though not always perfectly, in producing beneficial, lasting spiritual fruit for God's kingdom purposes. Therefore, the church bride of Christ, holy and dearly loved by our heavenly Bridegroom, is exhorted to, **"…put on compassion, kindness, humility, gentleness and patience" (Colossians 3:13)**. These God-honoring characteristics model our sovereign Savior and distinguish Christ-followers from the corrupt culture; yet it is the Holy Spirit who develops these biblical traits within believers and enables us to be burdened for unbelievers who need Jesus. Therefore, we continue to joyfully and urgently share the transforming gospel message of Jesus with others. Knowing the God of the Bible and resting in His marvelous mercy can help you experience God's plentiful peace, as expressed in **Psalm 46:10a, "Be still, and know that I am God" (ESV)**.

---

[15] Charles R. Swindoll, and J.I. Packer, "Knowing God," *The Tale of the Tardy Oxcart and 1,501 Other Stories* (Nashville, TN: Word Publishing, 1998), 236.

God's matchless mercy through His Son Jesus has the power to reach beyond borders, enable one to overcome obstacles, or break down barriers hindering an individual, so they may know and embrace the compassion of the Savior. The six women referenced within this *Nameless but Known* book dealt with problematic hurdles closely linked to divorce, disability, adultery, widowhood, motherhood, and an immoral, but forgiven past. Surprisingly, only one woman begged for mercy before the Son of God; most of them remained silent in His presence, but a couple of them have their spoken words to Jesus recorded in the Bible. Nevertheless, all six overlooked, desperate women were impacted by God's matchless mercy shown through acts of lovingkindness by Jesus.

Ironically, suffering and persevering through tests and trials provided the pathway for these diverse women to encounter the mercy and compassion of the same Savior. These biblical unknowns came to know Christ personally, even though He already knew each of them from their mothers' wombs. He changed their precious lives for the better, and their stories are still told today, even though the alphabet letters that form their individual names are never spelled out in Scripture. Perhaps silence is golden when it comes to role models like these and their faith response to Christ's mercy, since knowing the name of Jesus made the difference back then and still does today.

Pastor Paul David Tripp provides this reassuring wisdom: "…knowing God is so essential to everything we are and everything we are meant to do…Everything we need, we find in Him. Nothing is more important than knowing God…As we grow to know Him, we also grow in understanding the wonder of what it means to be known *by* Him."[16]

According to **John 1:1**, Jesus is the Word, so to know God's Word is to know Jesus. Let's keep seeking and studying God's truth found in the Bible, for only the Name of Jesus has been exalted by the Father above all other names, **"…so that at the Name of Jesus every knee will bow – in heaven and on earth and under the earth – and every tongue will confess that Jesus Christ is Lord, to the glory of God the Father"** (Philippians 2:9-11).

As we humbly bow before our compassionate Savior Jesus, and gratefully proclaim Him as our sovereign Lord, let's conclude by remembering the tremendous blessings spoken of throughout this book of God's matchless **MERCY** through Christ, who has the power to:

- Promise eternal **LIFE** for those who believe.
- Offer a **CHOICE** to repent of sin and follow Him.
- Summon **FAITH** in God and to trust His Word.
- Exhibit unfailing **LOVE** through forgiveness.
- Provide **FREEDOM** from bondage.
- Produce **HOPE** within sorrow amid death.

My prayer is that you will continue to grow in the grace and knowledge of Jesus, remembering that God's matchless mercy through Christ will change your life. So, how will you respond and who will you tell about it?

To God be the glory forevermore!

---

[16] Paul David Tripp, *Sunday Matters: 52 Devotionals to Prepare Your Heart For Church* (Wheaton, IL: Crossway, 2023), 227-228.

# Scripture Index

**Introduction**
Exodus 2:23-25
Psalm 139:1
Isaiah 49:13-16
Hebrews 4:16

**Chapter 1**
Exodus 34:6-7
Isaiah 46:5
Lamentations 3:22-23
Luke 6:31, 36
2 Corinthians 4:1
Ephesians 2:1-5
1 Timothy 1:15-16
Titus 3:4-5

**Chapter 2**
Deuteronomy 30:19-20
2 Chronicles 30:9
Psalm 36:9
Psalm 139:16
Proverbs 28:13
Isaiah 41:17
Isaiah 52:6-7
Isaiah 54:5-6
Malachi 2:15-16
Matthew 5:6, 31-32
Matthew 19:3-9
Luke 10:25-37
John 3:1-21
John 4:7-42
John 7:17, 38-39
Acts 1:8
Romans 3:29
Ephesians 2:12-14
Hebrews 4:15
James 5:11
1 Peter 3:8-9
2 Peter 3:9
1 John 1:1-3, 9
Revelation 21:2-3, 6

**Chapter 3**
Exodus 20:14
Leviticus 20:10
Deuteronomy 19:15
Psalm 19:12-13
Psalm 40:11-13
Psalm 142:3-5
Isaiah 50:9
Daniel 9:8-9
Matthew 5:27-28
Matthew 7:13-14
Matthew 18:15-17, 21-22
Mark 15:41
Luke 23:32-43
John 2:24-25
John 3:16-18
John 5:1-16
John 7:19
John 8:2-11
John 14:26-27
Romans 3:19-24
Romans 8:1-4, 34

Romans 10:10-11
Romans 13:1-7
1 Corinthians 6:9-11
1 Corinthians 10:13
Galatians 6:1
Ephesians 4:15
Colossians 2:13-15
James 5:19-20

**Chapter 4**
Exodus 3:7-10
Psalm 9:10
Psalm 28:6-7
Psalm 72:12-14
Psalm 116:1
Matthew 6:9-13
Matthew 15:21-28
Matthew 28:18
Mark 1:34
Mark 7:24-30
Mark 9:14-29
Luke 4:41
Luke 9:37-43
Luke 11:1, 9-10, 13
Luke 22:42
John 1:10-12
John 8:44
John 10:10
Romans 8:26-27

Ephesians 2:13-14
Ephesians 6:10-18
Philippians 2:3
Philippians 4:6-7
1 Timothy 4:1-2
James 2:19
James 4:7-8
James 5:15
1 John 5:19
Revelation 12:12
Revelation 18:2, 8

**Chapter 5**
Proverbs 10:12
Matthew 2:15-16
Matthew 18:23-35
Luke 6:27-36
Luke 7:34, 36-50
Luke 15:7
John 3:16-17
John 6:70-71
John 13:12-15, 34-35
Romans 2:4
Romans 5:6-8
Romans 12:18
2 Corinthians 7:10
Ephesians 1:7-8
Ephesians 4:32
2 Timothy 2:25
Hebrews 13:1-2

James 2:8-10
1 Peter 4:8
1 John 1:9
1 John 4:19

**Chapter 6**
Genesis 1:27
Exodus 4:11-12
Leviticus 21:16-23
Leviticus 26:13
1 Samuel 16:7
Job 1-2
Psalm 138:8
Psalm 139:13-16
Psalm 142:7
Isaiah 64:8
Matthew 9:18-22
Mark 5:21-34
Mark 9:20-21
Luke 6:5, 9
Luke 8:40-48
Luke 13:10-17
John 8:36
John 9:1-3
John 20:29
Romans 8:18, 20-21, 39
1 Corinthians 12:22-26
2 Corinthians 12:9
Ephesians 2:8-10
James 5:13, 16

1 Peter 5:10

**Chapter 7**
1 Kings 17:8-24
Psalm 56:13
Psalm 103:13
Ecclesiastes 3:14
Ecclesiastes 7:14
Isaiah 53:3
Lamentations 3:31-33
Mark 6:6
Luke 1:78-79
Luke 7:9, 11-17
John 19:26-27
Romans 15:13
2 Corinthians 1:3-4
Galatians 2:20
Galatians 6:2
Ephesians 4:1-3
1 Thessalonians 4:13-14
1 Peter 1:3
1 Peter 5:7

**Conclusion**
Psalm 46:10
Psalm 145:8-9
Proverbs 3:5-6
John 1:1
John 15:16
Acts 4:12
Romans 9:14-16

Philippians 2:9-11
Colossians 3:13

# About
# Kharis Publishing:

Kharis Publishing, an imprint of Kharis Media LLC, is a leading Christian and inspirational book publisher based in Aurora, Chicago metropolitan area, Illinois. Kharis' dual mission is to give voice to under-represented writers (including women and first-time authors) and equip orphans in developing countries with literacy tools. That is why, for each book sold, the publisher channels some of the proceeds into providing books and computers for orphanages in developing countries so that these kids may learn to read, dream, and grow. For a limited time, Kharis Publishing is accepting unsolicited queries for nonfiction (Christian, self-help, memoirs, business, health and wellness) from qualified leaders, professionals, pastors, and ministers. Learn more at:
https://kharispublishing.com/

www.ingramcontent.com/pod-product-compliance
Lightning Source LLC
Chambersburg PA
CBHW070201100426
42743CB00013B/2995